SOUTHERN MADE FRESH

Vibrant dishes rooted in homegrown flavor

TASIA MALAKASIS

Southern Living

CONTENTS

WELCOME

When I was young, I couldn't wait to leave Alabama—or so I thought. I wanted to travel and explore, to make my way in the world and find that special something that would define and fulfill me professionally. I was sure it was "out there" somewhere. As it turns out, while I spent 15 years forging a career as an Internet technologies executive, my special something was waiting, not in New York or Philadelphia or any of the urban centers where I had worked and traveled, but on a goat farm in pastoral Elkmont, Alabama.

In 2006, after many fast-paced years spent in and out of busy airports and boardrooms, I completely upended my life. By that time a single mom, I decided that my four-year-old and I would move home to Alabama, where I was planning to take a very big chance . . . on me. Why? Because I believed I had found something much more valuable than any job or career. I believed I had found my true vocation—my calling.

A little backstory: I'm blessed with a dual heritage in more ways than one. My father's family is Greek, but Mom's side is Southern to the core. So I've been steeped in not one but two food-loving cultures. Also, the two women who influenced me most as a young girl—my mom and her mother—offered up radically different definitions of "the Southern woman." My mom is very independent and modern. Her culinary repertoire includes all of two dishes—three at most. My grandmother, on the other hand, believed in cooking to show love. I think my love of cooking—of sharing great food with other people—comes from my grandmother, while the courage to blaze my own trail is likely a gift from Mom.

Even with that gift in hand, it took me years to make the leap from industry executive to cheesemaker. During a work sabbatical in the late 1990s, I took some classes at the Culinary Institute of America, where I learned, first and foremost, that I didn't want to be a chef. I had my son, Kelly, to raise, so working till 2 a.m. in a restaurant wasn't for me. Then one day, I went to Manhattan, specifically to shop at Dean & DeLuca. As I looked at cheeses from all over the world, I picked up one called Belle Chèvre, labeled "Made in Elkmont, Alabama." And then the heavens opened. Just kidding—it wasn't quite that dramatic, but it was definitely a moment.

For a while, I pushed that moment out of my mind. The siren's song of a big paycheck is tough to resist, and every time I would start to dream about Belle Chèvre, I would get one of those offers you can't refuse. Eventually, however, the pull of a different life, one that would allow me to follow my passion, was too strong to resist.

One day I just looked up and said, "I'm done." I called Belle Chèvre founder Liz Parnell and said, "Liz, I just quit my job, and I'm coming home to make cheese." For six months, I worked there for free, and then I bought the business in 2007.

The best part of my job is the creativity. We've developed a line of breakfast cheeses, which I think are wonderful, and we've made chèvre-iced cookies and an amazing goat cheese cheesecake. Why? Because we can, and they're good!

For me, food is about fun. It's what we do when we come together. It's how we love and heal and celebrate each other. It's also about inclusion. There's no such thing as a food you can't have for breakfast or an ingredient you must use in desserts only. Once you embrace this idea, the creative possibilities in your kitchen will be endless.

As I considered all the possibilities for *Southern Made Fresh*, I knew that I wanted everything in the book to be approachable. Americans today are fascinated with food, and we've elevated chefs to celebrity status, yet so many people are afraid to actually cook. I tell students in my cooking classes that there are only two rules: taste everything and have fun.

I also want this book to celebrate the South's rich agrarian heritage. For generations, Southern cooks planned their menus around what was fresh and in season, with homegrown fruits and vegetables, fish from local creeks and rivers, hand-churned butter, and eggs gathered from the henhouse the day they were laid. Thanks to the abundance of farmers' markets and other sources of fresh, whole foods in the South, you don't have to live on a farm to partake of this culinary bounty.

My personal journey has taught me that the South is the place on this planet that owns my heart. To paraphrase what T. S. Eliot writes so beautifully in my favorite poem, *Four Quartets*, when you are a convert, when you come back home to a place you once left so eagerly, you can embrace it and appreciate it in a way that you never could have before. That's what I want to celebrate in *Southern Made Fresh*—my deep appreciation for the South, its wonderful food, and the people who prepare it and share it with love.

Chapter

- 1 -

GOOD MORNING, Sunshine!

Bacon, Egg

I am a morning person who loves new beginnings.
And even though I know I'm not up for the daily
grind of restaurant ownership, I still harbor
fantasies of running a great little breakfast place.
There's just a world of opportunity for adventure
there. I can think of so many times when I've gone
to a wonderful breakfast restaurant and ordered
something absolutely crazy—something you never
would've imagined as the way to start your day.
From the minute I tried it, I wanted to shout,
"But of course!" In my grandmother's day—and
for generations before—breakfast was the hearty
meal that prepared farm families for long hours
of hard work in all kinds of weather. Fresh eggs
paired with homemade sausage, country ham, and
smoked bacon. And let's not forget those homemade
biscuits—light as a boll of cotton and slathered with
freshly churned butter and homemade preserves.
At the breakfast table, innovation and tradition
can meld together in a glorious way, taking
equal parts memory and discovery, and stirring
them up. Whether you choose pancakes or
spicy-savory favorites, you'll find simple, delicious
recipes you'll love in this chapter.

Bacon, Egg & Avocado
SANDWICHES

Just because it's a sandwich doesn't mean it's not perfect to serve at breakfast! A recipe this easy to prepare and take on-the-go is exactly what I'm looking for most mornings. A slice or two of ripe avocado turns it into something special.

serves: 4 ~ *hands-on:* 18 min. ~ *total:* 18 min.

4 large eggs

¼ tsp. table salt

¼ tsp. freshly ground black pepper

¼ cup mayonnaise

2 Tbsp. hot sauce

4 whole wheat English muffins, split and toasted

4 tsp. extra virgin olive oil

2 small green onions, chopped

8 cooked hickory-smoked bacon slices

1 ripe avocado, thinly sliced

1. Whisk together first 3 ingredients in a bowl. Stir together mayonnaise and hot sauce in a small bowl. Spread mayonnaise mixture evenly on cut sides of English muffins.

2. Heat oil in a small skillet over medium heat. Add green onions, and sauté 1 minute.

3. Add egg mixture to green onions, and cook, without stirring, 30 seconds or until egg mixture begins to set on bottom. Gently draw cooked edges away from sides of skillet to form large pieces. Cook, stirring occasionally, 1 minute or until eggs are thickened and moist. (Do not overstir.)

4. Place scrambled eggs evenly on mayonnaise mixture on bottom halves of English muffins. Layer bacon and avocado slices evenly over eggs. Cover with English muffin tops, cut sides down.

NOTE: We tested with Frank's RedHot Original Cayenne Pepper Sauce.

KITCHEN TIP

Don't overcook your scrambled eggs! As soon as they get close to finished, take the pan off the heat, and gently stir until they are done. They should still be soft and custardy.

Egg & Chorizo
QUESADILLAS

Mexican and South American food traditions heavily influenced me while growing up, and I often find myself incorporating ingredients like chorizo and cilantro into my recipes.

serves: 2 ~ *hands-on:* 16 min. ~ *total:* 16 min.

¼ tsp. table salt

¼ tsp. freshly ground black pepper

3 large eggs

2 tsp. olive oil

2 (8-inch) flour tortillas

4 oz. quesadilla cheese, shredded

5.3 oz. chorizo sausage (2 small links), cooked and crumbled

1 green onion, thinly sliced

Garnishes: sour cream, salsa, chopped green oinions, chopped cilantro

1. Whisk together first 3 ingredients. Heat oil in a medium skillet over medium heat. Add egg mixture to skillet, and cook, without stirring, 1 minute or until eggs begin to set on bottom. Gently draw cooked edges away from sides of skillet to form large pieces. Cook, stirring occasionally, 1 minute or until eggs are thickened and moist. (Do not overstir.) Transfer scrambled eggs to a small bowl; keep warm.

2. Heat a large cast-iron skillet over low heat until hot. Place 1 tortilla in skillet. Spoon egg mixture over tortilla; sprinkle with half of cheese, sausage, green onions, and remaining half of cheese, to within ½ inch of edge. Top with remaining tortilla, and cook over low heat 2 minutes on each side or until cheese melts.

This is my spin on eggs and sausage...griddled inside a tortilla for a spicy breakfast on the go.

Fried Eggs with Wilted
SPINACH SALAD

While some of us crave a sweet breakfast, I almost always long for something savory. Caramelized shallots and sautéed spinach cradling a crispy fried egg creates a satisfying plate of amazing flavor.

serves: 4 ~ *hands-on:* 10 min. ~ *total:* 20 min.

3 Tbsp. extra virgin olive oil, divided

4 large eggs

¼ tsp. freshly ground black pepper

⅛ tsp. kosher salt

4 thick hickory-smoked bacon slices

2 (6-oz.) packages fresh baby spinach

2 Tbsp. minced shallots

1 tsp. anchovy paste

1 small garlic clove, minced

4 tsp. sherry vinegar

1. Heat 1 Tbsp. oil in a large nonstick skillet over medium heat. Gently break eggs into hot skillet. Sprinkle eggs evenly with pepper and salt. Cook 2-3 minutes on each side or to desired degree of doneness. Remove from heat, and keep warm.

2. Cook bacon in a large cast-iron skillet over medium-high heat 5 minutes or until crisp; remove bacon, and drain on paper towels, reserving drippings in skillet.

3. Add half of spinach to hot drippings, and cook, stirring constantly, 1 minute or until spinach begins to wilt. Transfer to a large bowl. Repeat procedure with remaining spinach.

4. Add remaining 2 Tbsp. oil to skillet. Add shallots, anchovy paste, and garlic; sauté 30 seconds. Stir in vinegar. Pour dressing over spinach, tossing to coat. Divide spinach mixture among 4 plates. Top each serving with 1 fried egg, and place 1 bacon slice alongside. Serve immediately.

MARKET TIP

Two bags of fresh spinach might seem like gobs, but once it hits the skillet, it shrinks down tremendously. Trust me, you'll be glad you bought enough.

Mushroom & Green Onion
SCRAMBLE

Have you ever made an omelet, but with so many delicious additions it fell apart in a big heap? That's where a scramble comes in handy. Just add as many stir-ins as you like, and don't worry about it looking picture-perfect.

serves: 6 ~ hands-on: 14 min. ~ total: 29 min.

2 Tbsp. extra virgin olive oil

½ cup chopped green onions

1 (8-oz.) package fresh mushrooms, sliced

8 large eggs

½ cup milk

¾ tsp. table salt

¼ tsp. freshly ground black pepper

1 cup (4 oz.) freshly grated Parmesan cheese, divided

2 Tbsp. chopped fresh basil, divided

1. Heat oil in a 10-inch nonstick skillet over medium heat. Add green onions and mushrooms; cover, and cook, stirring occasionally, 8 minutes or until very tender.

2. Whisk together eggs, next 3 ingredients, ½ cup cheese, and 1 Tbsp. basil. Add egg mixture to mushroom mixture, and cook, without stirring, 2 minutes or until eggs begin to set on bottom. Gently draw cooked edges away from sides of skillet to form large pieces. Cook, stirring occasionally, 1-2 minutes or until eggs are thickened and moist. (Do not overstir.)

3. Sprinkle with remaining ½ cup cheese and remaining 1 Tbsp. basil. Serve immediately.

KITCHEN TIP

When using basil and other fresh herbs that bruise easily, I like to snip them with kitchen shears, letting the tender greens rain down like confetti.

Herbed Goat Cheese
FRITTATA

Frittatas are so easy to make and can be assembled with almost anything you have in your refrigerator. I make them for my son on most school mornings and give him a choice of what ingredients he'd like in them. Get the technique down, and you're free to play with your own variations.

serves: 8 ~ *hands-on:* 5 min. ~ *total:* 22 min.

2 Tbsp. chopped fresh basil

1 Tbsp. chopped fresh thyme

1 Tbsp. chopped fresh oregano

½ tsp. kosher salt

¼ tsp. freshly ground black pepper

12 large eggs

2 oz. Asiago cheese, shredded

6 oz. crumbled goat cheese, divided

1 tsp. extra virgin olive oil

1. Preheat oven to 400°. Whisk together first 6 ingredients; stir in Asiago cheese and half of goat cheese.

2. Heat oil in a 10-inch ovenproof nonstick skillet over medium heat. Add egg mixture, and cook, without stirring, 4 minutes or until edges are set. Sprinkle with remaining half of goat cheese.

3. Bake at 400° for 12 minutes or until set. Let stand 5 minutes. Cut into 8 wedges.

KITCHEN TIP

The frittata will still be mostly liquid when it is ready to be baked. Just make sure the edges are set up, and it will finish nicely in the oven.

Bacon, Tomato & Cheddar
FRITTATA

I like to think of frittatas as breakfast pizzas. You can choose your additions in the very same way you would choose your pizza toppings. Bacon, tomato, and Cheddar cheese taste divine with eggs, making an excellent start to your day (or ending, if you like breakfast for dinner).

serves: 6 ~ *hands-on:* 12 min. ~ *total:* 24 min.

1 Tbsp. extra virgin olive oil

2 cups grape tomatoes

1 cup thinly sliced green onions

½ tsp. coarse salt

¼ tsp. freshly ground black pepper

1 small garlic clove, minced

10 large eggs, lightly beaten

1 cup (4 oz.) shredded sharp Cheddar
   cheese

6 hickory-smoked bacon slices, cooked
   and crumbled

1 Tbsp. chopped fresh thyme, divided

1. Preheat oven to 425°. Heat oil in a 10-inch ovenproof nonstick skillet over medium-high heat. Add tomatoes and next 3 ingredients; sauté 5 minutes. Add garlic; sauté 1 minute.

2. Stir in eggs, cheese, bacon, and 1½ tsp. thyme. Cook, without stirring, 2 minutes or until edges are set.

3. Bake at 425° for 12 minutes or just until top is set.

4. Sprinkle remaining 1½ tsp. thyme over frittata; invert onto a plate. Cut into 6 wedges.

Whether brown, blue, or pure white,
fresh farmstand eggs can make all the
difference, especially in a frittata.

Spicy Andouille Spanish
TORTILLA

A Spanish tortilla has nothing at all to do with flour or masa tortillas we acquaint with tacos. In fact, it's most closely related to a frittata, but loaded with potatoes. Add some cheese, grape tomatoes, and a Vidalia onion, and you have a complete one-dish meal.

serves: 6 ~ *hands-on:* 50 min. ~ *total:* 50 min.

½ lb. andouille sausage*

2 Tbsp. olive oil

1 small sweet onion, vertically cut into thin slices

2 garlic cloves, minced

2 lb. Yukon gold potatoes, peeled and thinly sliced

1 tsp. table salt, divided

8 large eggs

¼ tsp. freshly ground black pepper

¾ cup grape tomatoes, halved

4 oz. Manchego cheese, shredded

Garnish: chopped green onions

1. Preheat oven to 350°. Cut sausage lengthwise in half; cut crosswise into ¼-inch-thick half-moon–shaped slices. Cook sausage in a 12-inch ovenproof skillet over medium-high heat, stirring occasionally, 5 minutes or until browned. Remove from skillet; drain on paper towels.

2. Heat oil in skillet over medium-high heat. Add onion, and sauté 5 minutes or until tender. Add garlic, and sauté 30 seconds. Stir in potato, ⅔ cup water, and ½ tsp. salt. Reduce heat to medium. Cover and cook, stirring occasionally, 10 minutes or until potatoes are tender and water has evaporated.

3. Whisk together eggs, pepper, and remaining ½ tsp. salt. Stir in sausage. Pour egg mixture over potato mixture in pan. Reduce heat to medium-low, and cook 4 minutes or until mixture begins to set. Sprinkle with tomato and cheese.

4. Bake, uncovered, at 350° for 5 minutes or until top is set. Turn oven to broil; broil 2 minutes or until cheese is golden and bubbly.

5. Slide tortilla onto a serving plate. Cut into 6 wedges.

*Spicy smoked sausage may be substituted.

WEEKEND
Brunch

SERVES 8

*Green Salad with Cheesy
Grits Croutons*

*Open-Faced Fried Egg Sandwiches
with Bacon & Chèvre*

Rhubarb Coffee Cake

Spicy Bloody Marys

On the weekends, I love taking time out to prepare a fantastic brunch with my son, Kelly, and our Great Dane, Belle, who somehow always joins in. And with neighbors often stopping by, all the more reason to sweeten up a full-blown breakfast with a fresh-from-the-oven rhubarb coffee cake!

Spicy Bloody Marys

Open-Faced Fried Egg
Sandwich with Bacon
& Chèvre

ENTERTAINING TIP

Create the perfect brunch salad:

- Turn cheesy grits into croutons by cutting into squares and baking or sautéeing
- Eggs, prepared any way, make a salad more satisfying
- Mild cheeses (goat cheese, feta, or mozzarella) add a hearty creaminess
- Top with crispy bacon, avocado slices, or fresh herbs

Rhubarb Coffee Cake

Green Salad with
Cheesy Grits Croutons

Green Salad with Cheesy Grits Croutons

serves: 8 ~ *hands-on:* 22 min.
total: 1 hr., 32 min.

CHEESY GRITS CROUTONS

2 cups reduced-sodium fat-free chicken broth

1 cup uncooked stone-ground grits

3 oz. herbed goat cheese

½ tsp. kosher salt

¼ tsp. freshly ground black pepper

2 Tbsp. vegetable oil

SALAD

2 tsp. red wine vinegar

½ tsp. Dijon mustard

¼ cup extra virgin olive oil

8 cups loosely packed torn green leaf lettuce

1. Prepare Croutons: Bring broth just to a boil in a large saucepan over medium-high heat; gradually whisk in grits. Reduce heat, and simmer, whisking constantly, 5 minutes or until grits are very thick. Remove from heat. Add cheese, salt, and pepper, stirring until cheese melts. Pour into an ungreased 8-inch square pan. Cover and chill 1 hour or until firm.

2. Preheat oven to 450°. Cut grits mixture into 1-inch squares. Place squares, in a single layer, on a jelly-roll pan; drizzle with 2 Tbsp. vegetable oil. Bake at 450° for 10 minutes. Turn squares over; bake 10 more minutes or until golden and crisp. Keep warm.

3. Prepare Salad: Whisk together first 2 ingredients in a large bowl. Gradually whisk in ¼ cup oil until blended. Add lettuce, tossing to coat. Season with salt and pepper, and sprinkle salad with warm croutons.

Open-Faced Fried Egg Sandwiches with Bacon & Chèvre

serves: 8 ~ *hands-on:* 12 min.
total: 12 min.

8 applewood-smoked bacon slices

8 large eggs

4 sourdough English muffins, split and toasted

2 oz. crumbled goat cheese

¼ cup chopped green onions (about 2 green onions)

1. Cook bacon in a large nonstick skillet over medium-high heat 6-8 minutes or until crisp; remove bacon, and drain on paper towels. Pour drippings from skillet; cut bacon slices in half.

2. Gently break 4 eggs into hot skillet, and season with salt and pepper. Cook 2-3 minutes on each side or to desired degree of doneness. Remove from pan; keep warm. Repeat procedure with remaining 4 eggs.

3. Place 2 half slices of bacon on cut sides of each muffin half. Top each with 1 egg. Sprinkle evenly with goat cheese and green onions.

Rhubarb Coffee Cake

serves: 15 ~ *hands-on:* 16 min.
total: 1 hr., 16 min.

CAKE

Butter

1 cup butter, softened

1 cup firmly packed light brown sugar

1 cup granulated sugar

2 extra-large eggs

1¾ cups buttermilk

1 tsp. vanilla extract

4 cups all-purpose flour

2 tsp. baking soda

½ tsp. table salt

2 cups chopped fresh rhubarb

2 Tbsp. all-purpose flour

TOPPING

½ cup firmly packed light brown sugar

¼ cup all-purpose flour

¼ cup butter, softened

1 tsp. ground cinnamon

1. Prepare Cake: Preheat oven to 350°. Lightly butter a 13- x 9-inch pan. Beat 1 cup butter and next 2 ingredients at medium speed with a heavy-duty electric mixer 3 minutes or until light and creamy. Add eggs, 1 at a time, beating just until blended after each addition. Add buttermilk and vanilla; beat at low speed 2 minutes, stopping to scrape bowl as needed.

2. Combine 4 cups flour, baking soda, and salt. Add one-third of flour mixture at a time to buttermilk mixture, beating at low speed just until blended after each addition. Toss together rhubarb and 2 Tbsp flour; fold into batter. Spread batter in prepared pan.

3. Prepare Topping: Stir together all ingredients in a small bowl until mixture resembles wet sand. Sprinkle topping evenly over batter.

4. Bake at 350° for 1 hour or until a wooden pick inserted in center comes out clean.

Spicy Bloody Marys

serves: 8 ~ *hands-on:* 7 min.
total: 2 hr., 7 min.

3½ cups tomato juice

1¼ cups vodka

2 Tbsp. chopped fresh cilantro

1 Tbsp. chopped fresh flat-leaf parsley

2 Tbsp. pimiento-stuffed Spanish olive juice

1 Tbsp. hot sauce

1 tsp. kosher salt

2 tsp. fresh or prepared horseradish

½ tsp. freshly ground black pepper

½ tsp. lime zest

3 Tbsp. fresh lime juice

1½ tsp. Worcestershire sauce

¼ tsp. celery salt

1 small jalapeño pepper, seeded and minced

Garnishes: pickled okra, celery stalks, pickled green beans, pimiento-stuffed Spanish olives

1. Combine all ingredients except garnishes in a pitcher, stirring well. Cover and chill at least 2 hours.

Grits with
RED-EYE GRAVY

This is probably the oldest recipe in my personal history. I grew up having red-eye gravy for breakfast with ham (or bacon) and eggs. Recalling my mother making red-eye gravy is a favorite childhood memory of mine.

serves: 4 ~ *hands-on:* 17 min. ~ *total:* 42 min.

GRITS

1¼ cups milk

1 tsp. table salt

1 cup uncooked stone-ground white grits

3 oz. goat cheese

RED-EYE GRAVY

2 Tbsp. bacon drippings, divided

3 (2-oz.) thin country ham slices

½ cup brewed coffee

2 Tbsp. butter

Garnish: green onion strips

1. Prepare Grits: Bring milk, salt, and 2 cups water to a boil in a 2-quart saucepan. Gradually whisk in grits; add goat cheese. Cook, whisking constantly, 1 minute or until cheese melts. Bring to a boil; cover, reduce heat, and simmer 25 minutes or until thickened, stirring in ¼ cup water halfway through. Remove from heat, and stir in ¼ cup water. Keep warm.

2. Meanwhile, prepare Red-Eye Gravy: Heat 1 Tbsp. bacon drippings in a medium skillet over medium heat. Add ham; cook, turning often, 5 minutes or until browned. Remove from skillet, and drain on paper towels.

3. Add remaining 1 Tbsp. bacon drippings to skillet. Add coffee and ¼ cup water; cook, stirring to loosen browned bits from bottom of skillet, 10 minutes. Add butter, stirring until melted.

4. Cut reserved ham into matchstick-size strips. Serve gravy over grits, and sprinkle with ham strips.

Sweet Potato
HASH

A hash is just another name for loaded breakfast potatoes. I like to make mine with sweet potatoes and a sprinkle of crushed red pepper to give them a kick. Serve this as a side, or mix in some crumbled breakfast sausage or bacon to make it a main dish.

serves: 4 ~ *hands-on:* 17 min. ~ *total:* 47 min.

2 large sweet potatoes (1¾ lb.), peeled and cut into ¾-inch cubes

4 thick hickory-smoked bacon slices

1 medium onion, cut into ⅓-inch-thick pieces

1 large garlic clove, minced

½ tsp. kosher salt, divided

¼ cup vegetable oil

¼ tsp. freshly ground black pepper

2 Tbsp. coarsely chopped fresh flat-leaf parsley

¼ tsp. dried crushed red pepper

1. Cook sweet potatoes in boiling salted water to cover 4-5 minutes or just until tender. Drain; rinse under cold running water. Drain. Chill 30 minutes or until cold.

2. Meanwhile, cook bacon in a large skillet over medium-high heat 6 minutes or until crisp; remove bacon, and drain on paper towels, reserving 2 Tbsp. drippings in skillet. Crumble bacon. Sauté onion, garlic, and ¼ tsp. salt in drippings 11 minutes or until onion is tender and golden brown. Transfer onion mixture to a small bowl.

3. Heat oil in skillet over medium-high heat. Add potato, black pepper, and remaining ¼ tsp. salt. Cook 11 minutes or until golden brown, stirring occasionally. Add reserved onion mixture; cook 2 minutes, stirring occasionally. Stir in bacon, parsley, and crushed red pepper. Serve immediately.

KITCHEN TIP

Get a head start on this dish by cooking and
chilling the sweet potatoes (step 1)
up to a day ahead.

Baked French Toast with
BANANA BRÛLÉE

This is the perfect dish to serve a crowd when you don't want to be chained to the kitchen but still want to impress. Prepare this the night before, and bake it in the morning while you relax over a cup of coffee.

serves: 8 ~ *hands-on:* 12 min. ~ *total:* 8 hr., 42 min.

1 cup buttermilk

1 cup milk

⅓ cup granulated sugar

1 Tbsp. Grand Marnier (optional)

½ tsp. ground cinnamon

⅛ tsp. freshly grated nutmeg

⅛ tsp. table salt

6 large eggs

1 (12-oz.) French bread loaf, cut into 16 (1½-inch-thick) slices

Butter

2 ripe bananas, sliced

⅓ cup firmly packed brown sugar

Maple syrup

1. Whisk together first 8 ingredients in a medium bowl. Dip bread slices on both sides into egg mixture. Place bread slices in a single layer in a buttered 13- x 9-inch baking dish. Pour remaining egg mixture over bread slices. Cover and chill overnight.

2. Preheat oven to 350°. Remove baking dish from refrigerator, and let stand while oven preheats. Uncover dish, and bake at 350° for 30 minutes or until set and bottom is lightly browned.

3. Remove baking dish from oven, and top French toast with banana slices. Sprinkle brown sugar over banana slices. Caramelize brown sugar using a kitchen torch, holding torch 1-2 inches from bananas and moving torch back and forth. Serve with maple syrup.

MARKET TIP

Choose the fat loaves of French bread for this dish—
you want something softer than a skinny baguette. Even
a loaf of Italian bread will work just fine.

Buttermilk Pecan
PANCAKES

There is nothing better than waking up to a weekend morning and the aroma of fresh pancakes, maple syrup, and sizzling bacon. It's the buttermilk that makes these pancakes fluffy and tender, and the cooked-in pecans add a nutty crunch.

serves: 4 ~ *hands-on:* 31 min. ~ *total:* 31 min.

2 cups unbleached all-purpose flour

3 Tbsp. sugar

1 tsp. baking powder

½ tsp. baking soda

½ tsp. table salt

2 large eggs, beaten

2 cups buttermilk

¼ cup unsalted butter, melted and cooled

Vegetable cooking spray

1 cup chopped toasted pecans

Maple syrup

Garnish: chopped toasted pecans

1. Whisk together first 5 ingredients in a large bowl.

2. Stir together eggs, buttermilk, and melted butter; add to dry mixture, stirring just until moistened.

3. Lightly grease a griddle with cooking spray or use a large nonstick skillet. Pour about ¼ cup batter for each pancake onto hot griddle or skillet. Sprinkle 1 Tbsp. pecans on top of each pancake. Cook pancakes over medium heat 3 minutes or until tops are covered with bubbles and edges look dry and cooked; turn and cook other side. Serve immediately with maple syrup.

KITCHEN TIP

If you have any leftover pancakes, freeze them in zip-top bags, and reheat in the toaster for an easy weekday breakfast.

Buttermilk Granola
MUFFINS

A muffin by itself might sound like a meager breakfast, but with the added granola these are surprisingly substantial.

makes: 1 dozen ~ *hands-on:* 8 min. ~ *total:* 31 min.

2 cups all-purpose flour

1 cup firmly packed light brown sugar

1 tsp. baking powder

½ tsp. baking soda

¾ tsp. table salt

2 cups Coconut-Pecan Granola (page 42), divided

1 large egg

1¼ cups buttermilk

⅓ cup vegetable oil

1 tsp. vanilla extract

Paper baking cups

1. Preheat oven to 400°. Combine first 5 ingredients and 1½ cups granola in a large bowl; make a well in center of mixture.

2. Whisk together egg and next 3 ingredients; add to dry mixture, stirring just until moistened. Place paper baking cups in a (12-cup) muffin pan. Spoon batter evenly into cups. Sprinkle with remaining ½ cup granola.

3. Bake at 400° for 18 minutes or until a wooden pick inserted in centers comes out clean. Cool in pans on wire racks 5 minutes. Remove from pans to wire racks. Serve warm, or cool completely (about 30 minutes).

These are perfect for sharing with a neighbor or a friend. Sometimes it's the simplest gesture that makes all the difference.

Coconut-Pecan
GRANOLA

Small Southern towns and landscapes are all dotted with pecan orchards. I was privileged to have family with a small orchard that we could walk through with a big paper bag and pick up the fallen goods to our hearts' content.

makes: 7½ cups ~ *hands-on:* 5 min. ~ *total time:* 1 hr., 50 min.

3 cups uncooked regular oats

1 cup unsweetened dried coconut flakes

1 cup pecans, coarsely chopped

½ cup pure maple syrup

½ cup extra virgin olive oil

½ cup firmly packed light brown sugar

¼ cup sesame seeds

1 tsp. kosher salt

¾ tsp. ground cinnamon

½ cup raisins

1. Preheat oven to 300°. Combine first 9 ingredients in a large bowl, stirring to coat.

2. Spread mixture in a lightly greased 17- x 12-inch jelly-roll pan.

3. Bake at 300° for 40 minutes, stirring at 10-minute intervals.

4. Stir in raisins. Bake 5 more minutes or until granola is golden brown. Cool completely in pan on a wire rack.

KITCHEN TIP

Don't overbake the granola. It might still seem wet or sticky, but it will firm up once it cools.

Brown Sugar–Glazed
BACON

Bacon is sooo back in fashion these days, free now from its long-standing prison of forbidden foods. Thank goodness, because there truly is no substitute for this classic American favorite. This recipe takes bacon to a whole new level with a sweet-and-spicy glaze that makes it exceptionally crispy. It's so delicious, I refer to it as bacon candy.

serves: 6 ~ ***hands-on:*** 4 min. ~ ***total:*** 59 min.

Parchment paper

Vegetable cooking spray

⅓ cup firmly packed light brown sugar

1½ tsp. freshly ground black pepper

1 lb. hickory-smoked bacon slices

1. Preheat oven to 375°. Line 2 (15- x 10-inch) jelly-roll pans with parchment paper. Set 1 wire rack coated with cooking spray in each pan. Combine brown sugar and pepper.

2. Arrange half of bacon slices on each rack. Bake at 375° for 10 minutes or just until bacon begins to curl.

3. Remove pans from oven, and sprinkle bacon with brown sugar mixture. Bake 30-35 more minutes or until bacon is crisp and brown. Remove from oven, and cool on wire racks 15 minutes before serving.

NOTE: We tested with Hormel Black Label Hickory Smoked Bacon.

KITCHEN TIP

By cooking the bacon on a rack in the oven, the fat drips away, leaving a super crunchy (and a bit healthier) result!

Garlic & Sage Breakfast
SAUSAGE

Making your own breakfast sausage is no more difficult than making a hamburger. Plus, you get to add more amazing flavor than what is in store-bought varieties. Don't forget the rubbed sage—it brings on that unmistakable robust sausage taste.

serves: 4 ~ *hands-on:* 15 min. ~ *total:* 15 min.

1 lb. ground pork

1 tsp. kosher salt

1 tsp. rubbed sage

½ tsp. dried thyme, crumbled

½ tsp. onion powder

½ tsp. freshly ground black pepper

¼ tsp. crushed red pepper

4 garlic cloves, minced

1 Tbsp. canola oil

1. Combine first 8 ingredients in a medium bowl. Divide pork mixture into 8 portions. Shape portions into 3-inch patties about ⅓ inch thick.

2. Heat oil in a large skillet over medium-high heat. Add patties, and cook 3 minutes. Reduce heat; turn patties over, and cook 3 more minutes or to desired degree of doneness. Drain on paper towels.

Some people swear by waking up to the aroma of coffee, but I'd argue that homemade sausage is a surefire way to wake up your entire household.

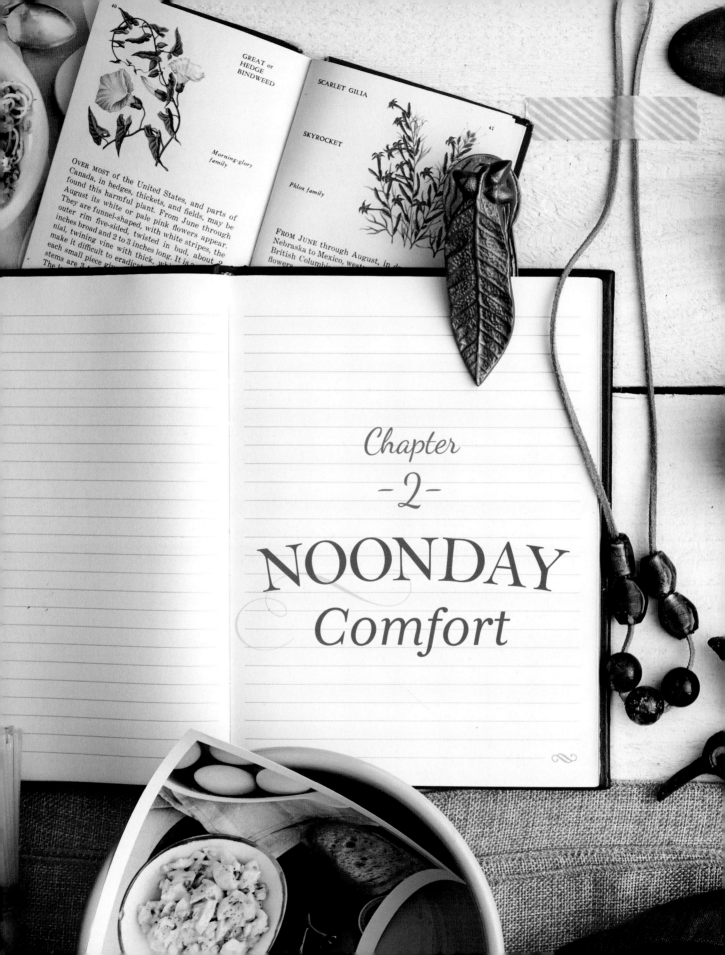

Chapter -2-

NOONDAY Comfort

There was a time, not so long ago, when Southern women raised the ladies' lunch to an art form. There would be finger sandwiches prepared just so, gazpacho and other elegant soups, deviled eggs, tomato aspic, and maybe red velvet cake for dessert, all served on fine china. I picture lovely clusters of camellias or gardenias on every table. Shalimar and White Shoulders wafting through the air. Hats and gloves all around. Alas, most of the busy women I know are wearing so many hats that they never have time to get dressed up in one. I have to confess that lunch is the one meal of the day to which I give very little thought. That's especially true when my son is in school and I have only to feed myself. The idea of just grabbing the same old sandwich or prefab deli salad brings me down. What I long for most at lunchtime is that sense of just-for-me. I want to take a midday break, not just to fill myself with whatever's quick and convenient, but to savor something I truly love. I want egg salad stirred together in my grandmother's mixing bowl, not hurriedly spooned from a plastic container. What I'm talking about, of course, is lunchtime comfort food, which doesn't have to mean fried chicken and macaroni and cheese.

Watermelon, Goat Cheese & Vidalia Onion
SALAD

These three ingredients may seem like strange friends, but the sweet watermelon, creamy goat cheese, and kick from the Vidalia make for an excellent combination!

serves: 12 ~ *hands-on:* 10 min. ~ *total:* 10 min.

2 tsp. fresh lemon juice

¾ tsp. table salt

¼ tsp. freshly ground black pepper

6 cups cubed watermelon, chilled

3 heirloom tomatoes (about 1½ lb.), cut into ½-inch wedges

1 large Vidalia or other sweet onion (about 1¼ lb.), cut into thin half-moon–shaped slices

1 (4-oz.) package crumbled goat cheese

½ cup firmly packed fresh basil leaves, torn

1. Whisk together first 3 ingredients in a large bowl. Add watermelon, tomato wedges, and onion; toss gently to coat. Sprinkle with goat cheese and basil.

MARKET TIP

A perfectly ripe watermelon makes all the difference. Look for dull, unblemished rind without cracks or soft spots.

Watercress & Apple SALAD

Madison County in Alabama, where I am from, was once known as the "Watercress Capital of the World." Watercress is grown in little ponds, which dot the area's landscape, and between 1900 and the 1960s, the county produced more than 2 million bunches. When I was a child, most of it was shipped off to the big cities like Chicago for use in fancy dishes. This recipe offers one way to enjoy this delicate Southern green.

serves: 6 ~ *hands-on:* 10 min. ~ *total:* 10 min.

2 Tbsp. extra virgin olive oil

1½ Tbsp. white wine vinegar

⅜ tsp. kosher salt

¼ tsp. freshly ground black pepper

3 cups torn frisée

1 large Granny Smith apple, cored and cut vertically into ¼-inch-thick slices

1 (4-oz.) package watercress

½ cup toasted pecan pieces

1. Whisk together first 4 ingredients in a large bowl. Add frisée and next 2 ingredients; toss to coat. Divide salad among 6 plates; sprinkle evenly with pecans.

A bunch of fresh watercress, whether snatched up from the creek or plucked off the produce shelves, gives this salad its cool, aromatic flavor.

SPRING GREENS
with Molasses, Bacon & Avocado

Molasses-glazed bacon bits are the star of this recipe. Their smoky-sweet crunch pairs perfectly with garden-fresh salads, but they can also bring a superb flavor to baked sweet potatoes.

serves: 6 ~ *hands-on:* 10 min. ~ *total:* 40 min.

6 thick hickory-smoked bacon slices

⅓ cup light molasses

½ tsp. freshly ground black pepper, divided

1 Tbsp. red wine vinegar

1 tsp. honey mustard

¼ tsp. sea salt

3 Tbsp. extra virgin olive oil

8 cups loosely packed torn salad greens

3 ripe avocados, cut into eighths

1. Preheat oven to 375° with oven rack positioned in top one-third of oven. Arrange bacon on a small baking sheet lined with aluminum foil. Brush molasses over bacon; sprinkle with ¼ tsp. pepper.

2. Bake at 375° for 30 minutes or until bacon is crisp. Transfer to a wire rack to cool.

3. Whisk together vinegar, next 2 ingredients, and remaining ¼ tsp. pepper in a large bowl until blended. Whisk in oil until blended.

4. Add greens to dressing, tossing to coat. Divide salad among 6 plates. Arrange 4 avocado wedges and crumble 1 bacon slice on top of each salad.

MARKET TIP

If your avocado isn't quite ripe, pop it into the microwave for about 10 seconds to help soften it up a bit.

RAW KALE SALAD
with Pecans & Parmesan Cheese

There has been a recent kale craze, and rightly so. It is not only healthy, but it can also be prepared in so many ways, including grilled, sautéed, raw, or baked as a snack. But don't eat it because it's healthy, eat it because it's delicious. This robust winter salad comes together in a snap, and it will instantly change your mind about the taste of kale.

serves: 4 ~ *hands-on:* 10 min. ~ *total:* 10 min.

SALAD

6 cups chopped curly kale

1 cup pecans, toasted and chopped

1 cup (4 oz.) freshly grated Parmesan cheese

DRESSING

½ cup olive oil

3 Tbsp. fresh lemon juice (1 lemon)

½ tsp. table salt

½ tsp. freshly ground black pepper

1. Prepare Salad: Combine kale, pecans, and cheese in a large bowl; toss well. Divide mixture among 4 plates.

2. Prepare Dressing: Combine oil, juice, salt, and pepper in a small jar. Cover with lid, and shake vigorously. Drizzle salads evenly with dressing.

MARKET TIP

When preparing fresh kale, be sure to remove the tough center rib of each leaf. Kale is a sturdy green, so it's ok to dress your salad up to an hour before serving it.

Celery–Apple SALAD

Celery doesn't get much attention in the kitchen it seems, but I love using the bright green stalks as well as the leaves. No need for lettuce here—the sprinkle of goat cheese and sliced green apples makes this vibrant salad refreshing and satisfying.

serves: 8 ~ *hands-on:* 28 min. ~ *total:* 28 min.

1 large bunch celery with leaves

1 tsp. orange zest

¼ cup fresh orange juice

¼ cup Dijon mustard

5 tsp. honey

½ tsp. table salt

½ tsp. freshly ground black pepper

⅔ cup grape seed oil

2 large Granny Smith apples, peeled, cored, and thinly sliced

½ cup pecans, toasted and chopped

3 oz. goat cheese, crumbled

1. Chop celery to measure 3⅓ cups and leaves to measure 1 cup; place in cold water to cover in a large bowl.

2. Whisk together orange zest and next 5 ingredients in a large bowl. Gradually whisk in oil.

3. Drain celery; pat dry with paper towels. Add celery, apple, and pecans to dressing, tossing to coat. Sprinkle with goat cheese.

KITCHEN TIP

Goat cheese is delectably creamy but can be messy to work with. It helps if you remove chilled goat cheese from the fridge just before crumbling.

Collard Green
COBB SALAD

There was a time when collards were considered the food you were limited to when money was tight. Now, they're experiencing the kind of attention they deserve and making their way onto fresh plates all over the country. Bravo, collards!

serves: 6-8 ~ *hands-on:* 28 min. ~ *total:* 28 min.

2 bunches collard greens, trimmed (about 20 oz.)

2 cups cherry tomatoes, halved

2 cups shredded carrot (about 4 carrots)

1 cup fresh corn kernels (about 2 ears)

4 hard-cooked eggs, peeled and diced

2 ripe avocados, diced

½ cup pecan halves, toasted

½ cup cooked and crumbled bacon

2 oz. crumbled goat cheese

Creamy Lemon-Garlic Dressing (page 67)

1. Chop collard greens to measure 6 cups; place greens in a large bowl. Add tomatoes and next 4 ingredients; toss well. Sprinkle with pecans, bacon, and cheese. Serve with Creamy Lemon-Garlic Dressing.

Grilled Vegetable
SALAD

I love to use my grill year-round, and not just for hamburgers and steaks. I grill fruits, vegetables, and even salads, because it's a great way to intensify the taste. The whole grain mustard dressing in this recipe brings all those flavors together.

serves: 6 ~ *hands-on:* 15 min. ~ *total:* 27 min.

1 Tbsp. red wine vinegar

2 tsp. minced shallot

1 tsp. whole grain mustard

¼ cup olive oil, divided

¾ tsp. kosher salt, divided

¾ tsp. freshly ground black pepper, divided

2 medium-size yellow squash, cut lengthwise into ¼-inch-thick slices

1 large red onion, cut into ½-inch-thick slices

1 large zucchini, cut lengthwise into ¼-inch-thick slices

1 large red bell pepper, seeded and cut into sixths

1 (8-oz.) package baby portobello mushrooms

1. Preheat grill to 350° to 400° (medium-high) heat. Whisk together first 3 ingredients, 2 Tbsp. oil, ¼ tsp. salt, and ¼ tsp. pepper in a small bowl.

2. Combine vegetables in a large bowl. Drizzle vegetables with remaining 2 Tbsp. oil; sprinkle with remaining ½ tsp. salt and ½ tsp. pepper.

3. Place vegetables, in 2 batches, on grill rack; grill, covered with grill lid, 3-4 minutes on each side or until tender.

4. Arrange vegetables on a platter, and drizzle with vinaigrette.

KITCHEN TIP

Keep an eye on the doneness of each vegetable as it cooks. The tender squash cooks quickly, and the firm red onion requires a bit more time.

Creamy Lemon-Garlic DRESSING

makes: 1⅔ cups ~ *hands-on:* 7 min. ~ *total:* 1 hr., 12 min.

½ cup fresh lemon juice (about 3 lemons)

1 tsp. kosher salt

2 garlic cloves, minced

2 tsp. Dijon mustard

1 cup heavy cream

¼ cup (1 oz.) freshly grated Parmesan cheese

1. Stir together first 3 ingredients. Let stand 5 minutes.

2. Whisk in mustard. Whisk in cream and cheese. Cover and chill 1 hour.

Ranch DRESSING

makes: 1 cup ~ *hands-on:* 4 min. ~ *total:* 4 min.

⅓ cup Greek yogurt

⅓ cup buttermilk

3 Tbsp. mayonnaise

2 Tbsp. finely chopped fresh chives

1½ tsp. fresh lemon juice (about 1 lemon)

1 tsp. Dijon mustard

½ tsp. table salt

½ tsp. onion powder

¼ tsp. garlic powder

1. Combine all ingredients in a medium bowl. Refrigerate in an airtight container.

BLT
with Avocado

Few things taste better in life than a BLT during the height of summer, when tomatoes are at their absolute peak. If I could be so brazen as to suggest any improvement to this timeless classic: Add an avocado to make this sandwich pure perfection.

serves: 4 ~ *hands-on:* 20 min. ~ *total:* 20 min.

½ cup mayonnaise

8 hearty multigrain bread slices, toasted

4 leaf lettuce leaves

1 large ripe tomato, cut into 8 thin slices

Kosher salt to taste

1 ripe avocado, cut into 12 slices

8 cooked thick hickory-smoked bacon slices

1. Spread 1 Tbsp. mayonnaise onto 1 side of each toast slice. Layer 1 lettuce leaf, 2 tomato slices (sprinkled evenly with salt to taste), 3 avocado slices, and 2 bacon slices on top of mayonnaise on 4 toast slices. Cover with remaining toast slices, mayonnaise sides down.

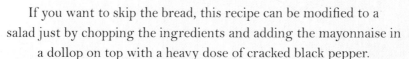

⟶ KITCHEN TIP ⟵

If you want to skip the bread, this recipe can be modified to a salad just by chopping the ingredients and adding the mayonnaise in a dollop on top with a heavy dose of cracked black pepper.

TEA SANDWICHES

Tea sandwiches are my favorite part of luncheon entertaining. It seems I only get them during dainty tea parties, but they are so much fun for any kind of get-together. Try them at tailgates and other casual events to take your menu up a notch.

Radish Tea Sandwiches

serves: 8 ~ *hands-on:* 40 min. ~ *total:* 40 min.

6 oz. goat cheese, softened

8 pumpernickel bread slices

4 large radishes, cut into thin half-moon–shaped slices

Kosher salt

Freshly ground black pepper

1. Spread goat cheese on 1 side of each bread slice. Layer 4 slices with slightly overlapping radish slices. Sprinkle lightly with salt and pepper. Top with remaining bread slices, goat cheese sides down.

2. Trim crusts from sandwiches using a serrated knife; cut each sandwich in half.

Smoked Salmon Tea Sandwiches

serves: 8 ~ *hands-on:* 40 min. ~ *total:* 40 min.

3 oz. cream cheese, softened

3 oz. goat cheese, softened

1 green onion, finely chopped

4 rye bread slices

6 oz. thinly sliced smoked salmon

½ cup torn watercress

1. Stir together first 3 ingredients in a small bowl until blended. Spread cheese mixture evenly over 1 side of bread slices. Layer salmon and watercress over cheese on 2 bread slices. Top with remaining 2 bread slices, cheese sides down.

2. Wrap sandwiches in plastic wrap; chill until firm.

3. Trim crusts with a serrated knife. Cut sandwiches diagonally in both directions to form 4 small triangles.

Ham Salad Tea Sandwiches

serves: 8 ~ *hands-on:* 40 min. ~ *total:* 40 min.

1 lb. smoked fully cooked boneless ham, cut into large chunks

½ cup mayonnaise

¼ cup sweet pickle relish

1½ tsp. celery seeds

¾ tsp. Dijon mustard

½ tsp. refrigerated horseradish

½ tsp. fresh lemon juice

⅛ tsp. seasoned pepper

16 thin white sandwich bread slices

1. Process ham in a food processor until coarsely ground, stopping to scrape down sides as needed. Place ground ham in a medium bowl. Stir in mayonnaise and next 6 ingredients.

2. Spread ham mixture evenly on 1 side of 8 bread slices. Top with remaining bread slices. Trim crusts from sandwiches using a serrated knife. Cut sandwiches in both directions to create 4 small squares.

Tomato Tea Sandwiches

serves: 8 ~ *hands-on:* 40 min. ~ *total:* 40 min.

3 Tbsp. mayonnaise

8 white sandwich bread slices

3 Tbsp. butter, softened

1½ tsp. chopped fresh parsley

1½ tsp. chopped fresh basil

2 plum tomatoes, thinly sliced

Sea salt

Freshly ground black pepper

1. Spread mayonnaise on 1 side of 4 bread slices. Stir together butter, parsley, and basil in a small bowl; spread evenly over 1 side of each remaining 4 bread slices. Layer tomato slices over butter mixture; sprinkle tomato with desired amount of sea salt and freshly ground pepper. Top with remaining bread slices, mayonnaise sides down.

2. Trim crusts from sandwiches using a serrated knife. Cut sandwiches diagonally in both directions to create 4 small triangles.

I long for those childhood lunches at my grandmother's house on Lake Guntersville in Alabama, where I could always count on a platter of sandwiches delivered to the dock when I went swimming with my friends.

EGG SALAD
for One

Egg salad served over some fresh greens or as a sandwich is one of my all-time favorites for a quick lunch. I like knowing I can make just one serving if I am looking for an easy and comforting meal. You can also make little tea sandwiches to serve as snacks at your next gathering by doubling or tripling this recipe.

serves: 1 ~ *hands-on:* 4 min. ~ *total:* 28 min.

2 large eggs

1 Tbsp. mayonnaise

1 tsp. minced celery

1 tsp. sweet pickle relish

½ tsp. Dijon mustard

¼ tsp. kosher salt

⅛ tsp. freshly ground black pepper

Dash of hot sauce

1. Place eggs in a small saucepan; add water to 1 inch above eggs. Bring to a boil; immediately remove from heat. Cover and let stand 12 minutes. Drain and return eggs to pan. Fill pan with cold water and ice; let stand 5 minutes or until eggs are thoroughly chilled.

2. Meanwhile, stir together mayonnaise and next 6 ingredients in a medium bowl. Tap each egg firmly on the counter until cracks form all over the shell. Peel under cold running water. Coarsely chop eggs, and fold into mayonnaise mixture.

Sometimes the easiest and simplest recipes have the most impact, like an egg salad sandwich on toasted bakery bread with a garden-ripe tomato slice.

CORN SALAD
with Radish

Corn is so amazingly versatile. Its subtle sweetness and ability to withstand a multitude of cooking techniques inspires me to incorporate it into most any recipe… stir-fried corn, cornbread, creamed corn, corn pudding… the list goes on! Without a doubt, it's the grilled corn in this salad that makes the dish memorable.

serves: 4-6 ~ ***hands-on:*** 20 min. ~ ***total:*** 28 min.

Vegetable cooking spray

4 ears fresh corn, husks removed

½ cup chopped red bell pepper

2 Tbsp. chopped fresh basil

2 Tbsp. mayonnaise

1 tsp. red wine vinegar

¾ tsp. kosher salt

½ tsp. freshly ground black pepper

6 radishes, cut into half-moon–shaped slices

Garnish: small fresh basil leaves

1. Preheat grill to 300° to 350° (medium) heat. Lightly grease a cold cooking grate with cooking spray, and place on grill. Place corn on cooking grate, and grill, covered with grill lid and turning occasionally, 8-10 minutes or to desired degree of doneness. Cut kernels from cobs, and place in a large bowl; discard cobs.

2. Add bell pepper and remaining ingredients (through radishes) to corn; toss well. Serve immediately, or cover and chill.

MARKET TIP

If you want to make your radishes "tamer," you can peel them. The radish peel is where most of the kick is, but it's also where all the beautiful color is! It's up to you.

Pimiento Chèvre
POTATO SALAD

A delicious way the French serve goat cheese is to melt fresh chèvre over steamed potatoes and top it with chives and herbs. I love the idea of giving that fun spin to potato salad with "pimiento chèvre."

serves: 8 ~ *hands-on:* 11 min. ~ *total:* 2 hr., 54 min.

2 Tbsp. kosher salt

3¼ lb. small white or yellow potatoes

¾ cup mayonnaise

½ cup chopped fresh chives

¼ cup chopped green onions

2 Tbsp. sherry vinegar

2 Tbsp. drained diced pimientos

1 tsp. minced garlic

1 tsp. kosher salt

1 tsp. freshly ground black pepper

6 oz. goat cheese, softened

1. Bring 2 Tbsp. salt, potatoes, and 2 qt. water to a boil in a Dutch oven; reduce heat, and simmer, uncovered, 20 minutes or until potatoes are almost tender when pierced with a sharp knife. Drain; cool 20 minutes or until cool enough to handle.

2. Halve or quarter potatoes to make uniform pieces; place in a large bowl.

3. Combine mayonnaise and remaining ingredients. Pour dressing over warm potatoes, stirring gently to coat. Cover and chill 2 hours to allow flavors to blend.

NOTE: We tested with Belle Chèvre goat cheese.

The subtle variation to this otherwise traditional dressing is almost undetectable. Your guests may not guess it's goat cheese, but they will love every bite.

BLT
Buttermilk Blue Slaw

My son eats only one type of lettuce. Even though I grow and bring home an abundance of beautiful tender varieties, he opts, always, for iceberg. This recipe is a great way to incorporate it into a tangy slaw. Add a sliced hard-cooked egg to make it a meal!

serves: 6 ~ *hands-on:* 15 min. ~ *total:* 15 min.

¼ cup buttermilk

3 Tbsp. mayonnaise

½ tsp. table salt

¼ tsp. freshly ground black pepper

½ cup crumbled blue cheese

½ cup thinly sliced red onion

3 Tbsp. coarsely chopped fresh parsley

1 lb. multicolored baby heirloom
   tomatoes, cut into thin wedges

1 head iceberg lettuce (about 1½ lb.),
   quartered and shredded

5 applewood-smoked bacon slices,
   cooked and crumbled

1. Stir together first 4 ingredients in a bowl. Gently stir in cheese.

2. Combine onion and next 3 ingredients in a large bowl. Drizzle dressing over lettuce mixture; sprinkle with bacon, and toss gently. Serve immediately.

> ⌐ KITCHEN TIP ⌐
>
> Don't have any buttermilk on hand? Don't fret!
> It's so easy to create your own. Just add ¼ cup of vinegar
> to a cup of milk and let it stand for 10-15 mins. Voilà!

Brussels Sprouts
SLAW

As a child, I thought that Brussels sprouts were the most wretched form of punishment thought up to torture children. Looking back, I think it was less of the sprouts' fault and more of the cook's (No offense to my mother!). Now I love them prepared all sorts of ways—roasted, sautéed, or shredded in a savory slaw.

serves: 4-6 ~ *hands-on:* 15 min. ~ *total:* 15 min.

2 Tbsp. fresh lemon juice (about 1 large lemon)

1 tsp. honey

1 tsp. whole grain mustard

¼ tsp. table salt

¼ tsp. freshly ground black pepper

1 Tbsp. olive oil

3 cups large Brussels sprouts

3 green onions, chopped

½ cup (2 oz.) freshly grated Parmesan cheese

1. Whisk together first 5 ingredients in a small bowl. Whisk in oil until blended.

2. Remove discolored leaves from Brussels sprouts; cut off and discard stem ends. Cut Brussels sprouts in half, and then cut each half crosswise into thin slices.

3. Place Brussels sprouts and green onions in a bowl; add dressing, and toss to coat. Sprinkle with cheese; toss. Cover and chill until ready to serve.

If you still have doubts about Brussels sprouts, this recipe will definitely change your mind!

LUNCH
Date

SERVES 4

Sun Drop Cocktail

Gazpacho

Shrimp Burgers

Peas & Radish Salad

It doesn't take more than some pretty glassware, a vase of peonies, and a delicious drink to turn sandwiches into a special occasion. Place the drinks on a side table, and you have a chic, impromptu bar cart that transforms a casual lunch into a celebration.

Sun Drop Cocktail

Peas & Radish Salad

Shrimp Burgers

Gazpacho

ENTERTAINING TIP

Stock the perfect bar cart with:

- Stylish cocktail stirrers and crisp linen napkins
- A sizeable ice bucket filled with crushed ice
- An array of sparkling glassware or crystal stemware
- A plate of fresh lemon and lime slices
- Your favorite signature spirits and liqueurs

Sun Drop Cocktail

serves: 1 ~ *hands-on:* 5 min.
total: 5 min.

½ *cup pink lemonade*

¼ *cup vodka*

2 *Tbsp. lemon-lime soft drink*

Garnish: 1 lemon slice

1. Combine lemonade and vodka in a tall glass filled with ice, stirring gently to blend. Top with lemon-lime soft drink.

NOTE: We tested with Sprite.

Citrus-flavored Sun Drop seems to be the official soft drink of Elkmont, Alabama, but it isn't available everywhere. Replicate its unique taste with this refreshing beverage—with or without the vodka.

Gazpacho

makes: 8 cups ~ *hands-on:* 15 min.
total: 45 min.

6 *Tbsp. sherry vinegar*

¼ *cup coarsely chopped fresh parsley*

¼ *cup extra virgin olive oil*

2 *Tbsp. fresh lime juice (about 1 large lime)*

1½ *tsp. table salt*

1 *tsp. hot sauce*

3 *lb. plum tomatoes, coarsely chopped*

2 *garlic cloves, peeled*

1 *cucumber, peeled, seeded, and coarsely chopped*

1 *yellow bell pepper, seeded and coarsely chopped*

1 *(5.5-oz.) can spicy vegetable juice*

½ *jalapeño pepper, seeded*

3 *Tbsp. sour cream*

1 *(4-oz.) goat cheese log*

Toasted French bread slices

1. Combine first 12 ingredients and 2 cups water in a large bowl. Process half of vegetable mixture in a food processor until smooth. Pour into a bowl; repeat procedure with remaining half of vegetable mixture. Cover and chill at least 30 minutes.

2. Stir together sour cream and goat cheese until blended. Serve gazpacho with a dollop of goat cheese mixture and toasts.

Shrimp Burgers

serves: 4 ~ *hands-on:* 20 min.
total: 20 min.

1 lb. large shrimp, peeled, deveined, and
   coarsely chopped

⅓ cup plus 4 Tbsp. mayonnaise, divided

3 Tbsp. chopped green onions (about
   1 green onion)

1 tsp. Old Bay seasoning

1 tsp. lemon zest

1 tsp. Dijon mustard

½ tsp. table salt

¼ tsp. freshly ground black pepper

⅛ tsp. ground red pepper

1 Tbsp. fresh lemon juice (about 1 lemon)

1 large egg

1½ cups panko (Japanese breadcrumbs),
   divided

¼ cup peanut oil

⅓ cup mayonnaise

1½ tsp. Asian hot chili sauce (such as Sriracha)

4 hamburger buns, toasted

*Garnishes: pickled okra, sliced lengthwise,
   tomato slices, lettuce leaves*

1. Prepare Burgers: Combine shrimp, 4 Tbsp.
mayonnaise, and next 9 ingredients. Stir in
¾ cup panko. Place remaining ¾ cup panko
in a shallow dish. Shape shrimp mixture into
4 (3½-inch) patties. Dredge patties in panko.

2. Heat 2 Tbsp. oil in a large heavy skillet over
medium-high heat. Fry patties in hot oil 3 minutes on each side or until golden brown and to
desired degree of doneness, adding remaining
2 Tbsp. oil as needed for even browning.

3. Stir together remaining ⅓ cup mayonnaise
and hot chili sauce in a small bowl. Spread
mayonnaise mixture evenly on bottom of
each bun. Place 1 shrimp patty on top of
mayonnaise mixture. Cover with top of bun.

Peas & Radish Salad

serves: 6 ~ *hands-on:* 15 min.
total: 15 min.

1 lb. fresh green peas*

8 radishes, cut into half-moon–shaped slices

2 Tbsp. olive oil

½ tsp. lemon zest

2 Tbsp. fresh lemon juice (about 1 large lemon)

½ tsp. kosher salt

½ tsp. freshly ground black pepper

1. Cook peas in boiling water to cover
1–3 minutes or until crisp-tender; drain.
Plunge into ice water to stop the cooking
process; drain.

2. Combine peas and radishes in a medium
bowl. Stir together olive oil and next 4 ingredients in a small bowl; add to pea mixture,
tossing to coat. Serve immediately.

**You may substitute 1 lb. frozen green peas,
thawed, for fresh peas, if desired.*

PEA SOUP
with Pesto Crostini

The vibrant color of this soup is matched only by its dynamic fresh taste! The accompanying pesto crostini complement the earthy flavor of the sweet peas and elevate the dish to a homemade specialty.

makes: 6½ cups ~ *hands-on:* 7 min. ~ *total:* 16 min.

PEA SOUP

1¾ cups canned reduced-sodium fat-free chicken broth

1 cup finely chopped onion

½ cup thinly sliced carrot

¾ tsp. table salt

¼ tsp. freshly ground black pepper

1 (16-oz.) package frozen baby sweet peas, thawed

½ cup whipping cream

¼ cup Pecan Pesto (page 96)

PESTO CROSTINI

6 (¼-inch-thick) diagonally-cut French bread baguette slices, toasted

3 oz. goat cheese

2 Tbsp. Pecan Pesto (page 96)

1. Prepare Pea Soup: Bring first 5 ingredients and 2 cups water to a boil in a medium saucepan; reduce heat, cover, and simmer 6 minutes or until vegetables are tender.

2. Add peas, and return to a boil; reduce heat, and simmer, uncovered, 3 minutes or until peas are bright green. Stir in cream and ¼ cup Pecan Pesto. Process half of soup in a blender until smooth; pour into a large bowl. Process remaining half of soup. Return soup to saucepan; keep warm.

3. Prepare Pesto Crostini: Spread toasted baguette slices with goat cheese, and top each with 1 tsp. Pecan Pesto. Refrigerate in an airtight container.

KITCHEN TIP

Once all the soup is pureed, you can adjust it to a desired thickness by slowly adding some additional chicken broth.

SUMMER CORN SOUP
with Corn Salsa

I love that this creamy soup is deceivingly thick, even though it has no cream in it at all. Use any extra soup stock, which is made from the corn cobs, in other vegetable-based soups.

makes: 5 cups soup, 1 cup salsa ~ **hands-on:** 1 hr., 12 min. ~ *total:* 1 hr., 12 min.

5 ears fresh corn

1½ tsp. table salt, divided

2 Tbsp. extra virgin olive oil, divided

2 Tbsp. chopped red onion

2 Tbsp. chopped fresh cilantro

2 Tbsp. fresh lime juice (about 2 limes)

½ tsp. sugar

½ small jalapeño pepper, seeded and diced

1½ cups chopped white onion

2 garlic cloves, minced

Garnish: chopped fresh cilantro or chopped fresh chives

1. Cut corn kernels from cobs to measure 5 cups, and place in a bowl, reserving cobs. Place corn cobs, 6 cups water, and ½ tsp. salt in a Dutch oven. Bring to a boil; reduce heat, partially cover, and simmer 30 minutes.

2. Meanwhile, heat 1 tsp. oil in a small saucepan over medium-high heat. Add 1 cup corn kernels; sauté 5 minutes or

until tender and beginning to brown. Transfer to a small bowl, and add red onion, next 4 ingredients, 2 tsp. oil, and ½ tsp. salt, stirring well. Cover corn salsa, and let stand until ready to serve.

3. Remove and discard cobs from corn stock. Pour stock through a fine wire-mesh strainer into a bowl to measure 3 cups.

4. Heat remaining 1 Tbsp. oil over medium heat in a large saucepan. Add white onion; sauté 5 minutes. Add garlic; sauté 30 seconds. Add remaining 4 cups corn kernels and remaining ½ tsp. salt. Cook, stirring often, 4–5 minutes or just until corn is tender. Add stock; bring to a simmer; cover and simmer 15 minutes.

5. Place half of soup in a blender. Remove center piece of blender lid (to allow steam to escape); secure lid on blender. Place a clean towel over opening in lid (to avoid splatters). Blend until smooth; pour into a large bowl. Repeat procedure with remaining half of soup.

6. Return soup to pan, and cook over medium-high heat 2 minutes or until thoroughly heated. Ladle soup into bowls. Top with corn salsa.

Classic Tomato
SOUP

Soup is my comfort food. The ladies who work with me at Belle Chèvre know that if I have brought soup for lunch, I am seeking something special from my meal—well beyond just satisfying hunger. My grandmother used to make me tomato soup, so this recipe packs a double punch of comfort for me.

makes: 14½ cups ~ *hands-on:* 16 min. ~ *total:* 1 hr., 1 min.

2 Tbsp. butter

2 cups finely chopped onion

3 garlic cloves, minced

5¼ cups canned reduced-sodium fat-free chicken broth

1 tsp. dried oregano

3 (28-oz.) cans crushed tomatoes

½ cup half-and-half

½ tsp. table salt

½ tsp. freshly ground black pepper

Garnishes: small fresh basil leaves, croutons

1. Melt butter in a Dutch oven over medium-low heat. Add onion and garlic; sauté 6 minutes or until tender.

2. Add broth and next 2 ingredients. Bring to a boil; reduce heat, and simmer, uncovered, 45 minutes or until thickened.

3. Slowly stir in half-and-half, salt, and pepper.

KITCHEN TIP

You can adjust this classic recipe to suit your taste by either leaving out the half-and-half entirely or by doubling it for an extra creamy consistency.

VEGETABLE SOUP
with Pecan Pesto

There are a million different vegetable soups out there, and I feel they should really complement the season. In the warmer months, soups should be light and refreshing, like this one packed with zucchini and tomatoes. In the cooler months, I want a rich and hearty soup that sticks to the bones.

makes: 14 cups ~ *hands-on:* 40 min. ~ *total:* 40 min.

2 leeks

1 Tbsp. olive oil

1½ cups chopped red onion

1⅓ cups sliced celery

2½ cups (½-inch) cubed peeled potatoes

6 cups vegetable broth

4 plum tomatoes, peeled, seeded, and cut into ½-inch pieces

2 medium zucchini, quartered and sliced into ½-inch pieces

2 (16-oz.) cans white beans, drained and rinsed

½ cup frozen baby sweet peas

¾ tsp. table salt

¼ tsp. freshly ground black pepper

½ cup Pecan Pesto

1. Remove and discard root ends and dark green tops of leeks. Cut in half length-wise, and rinse thoroughly under cold running water to remove grit and sand; drain. Slice leeks.

2. Heat 1 Tbsp. oil in a Dutch oven over medium heat. Add onion, celery, and leeks; sauté 6 minutes or until almost tender. Add potato and broth. Bring to a boil; cover, reduce heat, and simmer 10 minutes or until potato is almost tender.

3. Add tomatoes, zucchini, and beans to soup; cook 5 minutes. Add peas, salt, and pepper; cook 2 minutes or until thoroughly heated.

4. Ladle soup into 8 bowls. Top each serving with 1 Tbsp. Pecan Pesto.

Pecan Pesto

makes: about 1 cup ~ *hands-on:* 5 min. *total:* 5 min.

1 large garlic clove, peeled

2 cups loosely packed fresh basil leaves

1 cup (4 oz.) freshly grated Parmesan cheese

¼ cup toasted pecans

½ tsp. table salt

½ cup extra virgin olive oil

1. With processor running, drop garlic through food chute; process until minced. Add basil and next 3 ingredients; process until smooth. With processor running, pour oil through food chute; process until pesto is blended. Refrigerate in an airtight container.

Creamy Zucchini
SOUP

I have a friend who grows zucchini in her garden every year and is always so overrun with it that she will deliver bushels straight to my front door—sometimes in the middle of the night just to relieve the burden of her bounty. What a gift…and with it, I love returning the favor with this delicious soup!

makes: 8 cups ~ *hands-on:* 32 min. ~ *total:* 32 min.

3 Tbsp. olive oil

1 small onion, diced

4 garlic cloves, minced

6 large zucchini (about 3½ lb.), cut into ½-inch pieces

2 cups vegetable broth

½ cup heavy cream

1¼ tsp. table salt

½ tsp. freshly ground black pepper

½ cup (2 oz.) freshly grated Parmesan cheese

Garnish: chopped fresh chives

1. Heat 3 Tbsp. olive oil in a 6-quart Dutch oven over medium-high heat. Add onion, and sauté 5 minutes or until tender. Add garlic; sauté 30 seconds. Add zucchini; cook, stirring occasionally, 15 minutes or until tender.

2. Stir in broth and ½ cup water. Bring to a boil; reduce, heat, and simmer, uncovered, 5 minutes. Remove from heat.

3. Process one-third of soup in a blender until smooth; pour into a large bowl. Repeat procedure twice with remaining soup. Stir in cream, salt, and pepper. Return soup to Dutch oven; cook, stirring constantly, over medium heat 1 minute or until thoroughly heated. Ladle soup into bowls, and sprinkle evenly with Parmesan cheese.

MARKET TIP

At the market, choose small zucchini with brightly colored, blemish-free skins. Refrigerate them in plastic bags for no more than five days.

ONION SOUP
with Bacon

My version of onion soup gets an extra punch of flavor from smoky bacon. If you can ever get your hands on Allan Benton's bacon out of East Tennessee, you will be oh-so glad you did.

makes: 6 cups ~ *hands-on:* 1 hr., 15 min. ~ *total:* 1 hr., 15 min.

6 hickory-smoked bacon slices, cut crosswise into 1-inch pieces

¼ cup butter

3 large yellow onions, cut vertically into thin strips

⅔ cup ruby port

4 cups low-sodium beef broth

¼ tsp. table salt

¼ tsp. freshly ground black pepper

12 (½-inch-thick) French bread baguette slices

8 oz. Gruyère cheese, shredded

KITCHEN TIP

Don't rush the onions! Depending on the heat of your stove, they may take longer to develop their caramel color, but it is absolutely worth it.

1. Cook bacon in a 6-quart Dutch oven over medium-high heat, stirring occasionally, 6 minutes or until crisp. Remove bacon, and drain on paper towels, reserving 2 Tbsp. drippings in Dutch oven.

2. Melt butter with drippings over medium heat. Add onion strips, and cook, stirring occasionally, 4-5 minutes or until golden brown.

3. Add port, and cook, stirring to loosen browned bits from bottom of Dutch oven, 2 minutes or until reduced slightly. Add beef broth, salt, and pepper. Bring to a boil; reduce heat, and simmer, uncovered, 5 minutes.

4. Preheat broiler with oven rack 6 inches from heat.

5. Ladle soup into 6 (8-oz.) broiler-proof bowls or crocks. Place bowls on a baking sheet. Top each with 2 baguette slices; sprinkle evenly with bacon and cheese.

6. Broil 3 minutes or until cheese is melted and bubbly. Serve immediately.

Collard & Black-Eyed Pea
SOUP

makes: 18 cups ~ *hands-on:* 1 hr., 44 min. ~ *total:* 2 hr., 44 min.

8 cups vegetable broth

2 cups dry white wine

4 carrots, coarsely chopped

4 celery ribs, coarsely chopped

2 large onions, coarsely chopped

20 oz. smoked ham hocks

1 bay leaf

1½ tsp. table salt, divided

15 to 20 parsley sprigs

1 large garlic bulb

1 (1-lb.) package dried black-eyed peas

1 (1½-lb.) bunch collard greens, washed,
  trimmed, and coarsely chopped

½ tsp. freshly ground black pepper

8 oz. bakery cornbread

2 oz. goat cheese, softened

Accompaniments: cider vinegar, liquid
  from hot peppers in vinegar

1. Place first 7 ingredients, 3 cups water, and 1 tsp. salt in a large stockpot. Tie parsley sprigs together with kitchen string; add to stockpot. Scrub root end of garlic bulb, and rinse well. Cut off pointed end of garlic; add bulb to stockpot. Bring to a boil; reduce heat to medium-low, and simmer, uncovered and stirring occasionally, 1 hour.

2. While vegetables and ham simmer, rinse and sort peas according to package directions. Place peas in a Dutch oven; cover with water to 2 inches above peas. Bring to a boil. Boil 2 minutes; cover, remove from heat, and let stand 1 hour. Drain.

3. Add greens to stockpot. Return to a boil; reduce heat, partially cover, and simmer 15 minutes or until greens wilt. Add peas; bring to a simmer. Cover and cook 45 minutes or until peas are tender.

4. Remove and discard parsley and bay leaf. Remove ham hocks and garlic. Using a slotted spoon, transfer 4 cups of vegetable and pea mixture to a food processor; add ½ cup soup broth. Squeeze pulp from garlic bulb, and add to food processor. Process until smooth, scraping down sides if necessary. Return pureed vegetable mixture to Dutch oven.

5. Remove meat from bones; discard bones. Chop meat, and return to soup. Stir in pepper and remaining ½ tsp. salt.

6. Preheat broiler with oven rack 4 inches from heat. Cut cornbread into 2-inch squares, ¼ inch thick. Place on a baking sheet. Broil 1 minute on each side or until lightly browned and crisp.

7. Spread goat cheese on cornbread croutons. Ladle soup into bowls, and top with croutons. Serve with desired accompaniments.

Smoked Sausage & Kale
SOUP

By the time it really begins to feel like fall in Alabama, it's well into October, and the leaves are just thinking about turning colors. The slight chill in the air always inspires me to cook up a big pot of soup like this one, packed with hearty vegetables and smoky andouille.

makes: 17 cups ~ *hands-on:* 53 min. ~ *total:* 53 min.

12 oz. andouille sausage

1 Tbsp. olive oil

1 onion, diced

1 tsp. dried oregano

¼ tsp. dried crushed red pepper

4 garlic cloves, minced

½ cup dry white wine

5½ cups canned reduced-sodium fat-free chicken broth

1½ lb. potatoes, peeled and cut into ½-inch chunks

2 (14.5-oz.) cans diced tomatoes, undrained

1 bunch kale (about 12 oz.)

1 (16-oz.) can navy beans, drained and rinsed

1 tsp. table salt

1. Cut sausage in half lengthwise, and then cut crosswise into ¼-inch half-moon–shaped slices.

2. Sauté sausage in a large Dutch oven over medium-high heat 6 minutes or until browned; drain on paper towels, and discard drippings in Dutch oven. Heat oil in Dutch oven over medium-high heat. Add onion; sauté 4 minutes. Add oregano and next 2 ingredients; sauté 1 minute. Add wine, and cook, stirring to loosen browned bits from bottom of skillet, 1 minute. Add broth, potato, and tomatoes. Bring to a boil; reduce heat, and simmer, uncovered, 10 minutes or until potato is almost tender.

3. Meanwhile, trim and discard tough stalks from center of kale leaves; chop to measure 8 cups.

4. Process half of soup in a blender until smooth. Return pureed soup to Dutch oven. Add kale; bring to a simmer, and cook, uncovered, 5 minutes or until kale wilts. Stir in sausage, beans, and salt. Simmer, uncovered, 5 minutes or until thoroughly heated.

TOMATO PIE
with Fresh Corn & Herbs

A tomato pie is a delicious creation—almost as good as the first tomato sandwich of the season. Every summer, I look forward to it. If you've never heard of a tomato pie, think of it as an eggless quiche. Trust me, it will become your new favorite.

serves: 6 ~ hands-on: 20 min. ~ total: 3 hr., 41 min.

½ recipe *Basic Pie Crust (page 281)*

2 lb. *heirloom tomatoes, thinly sliced*

1½ tsp. *kosher salt, divided*

½ cup *mayonnaise*

1 Tbsp. *fresh lemon juice (1 lemon)*

1 cup (4 oz.) *finely shredded Parmesan cheese, divided*

1½ cups *fresh corn kernels (2 ears), divided*

2 Tbsp. *finely chopped fresh basil, divided*

1 Tbsp. *finely chopped fresh chives, divided*

¼ tsp. *freshly ground black pepper, divided*

1. Prepare Pie Crust: Preheat oven to 425°.

2. Roll Basic Pie Crust dough into a 12-inch circle on a lightly floured surface. Fit pastry into a 9-inch pie plate; fold edges under, and crimp. Line pastry with aluminum foil; fill with pie weights or dried beans (this will keep the crust from bubbling up).

3. Bake at 425° for 20 minutes. Remove weights and foil, and bake 5 more minutes or until browned. Cool completely on a wire rack (about 30 minutes). Reduce oven temperature to 375°.

4. Place tomatoes in a single layer on paper towels; sprinkle with 1 tsp. salt. Let stand 10 minutes.

5. Whisk together mayonnaise, lemon juice, and ¾ cup cheese in a small bowl.

6. Sprinkle ¾ cup corn in bottom of crust; sprinkle with 1 Tbsp. basil, 1½ tsp. chives, ¼ tsp. salt, and ⅛ tsp. pepper. Pat tomatoes dry with a paper towel.

7. Arrange half of tomato slices over corn, overlapping slightly. Repeat layering with remaining ¾ cup corn, remaining 1 Tbsp. basil, remaining 1½ tsp. chives, remaining ¼ tsp. salt, and remaining ⅛ tsp. pepper. Spread mayonnaise mixture over filling. Arrange remaining tomatoes over mayonnaise mixture, overlapping slightly. Sprinkle with remaining ¼ cup Parmesan cheese.

8. Bake at 375°, shielding crust with aluminum foil to prevent excessive browning, for 1 hour or until filling is bubbly and cheese melts. Let stand on a wire rack 15 minutes before cutting into wedges. Serve warm or at room temperature.

PASTA
with Green Tomatoes & Goat Cheese

If you or a generous neighbor is knee-deep in green tomatoes by late summer, you can use them up in a variety of dishes. Think beyond the classic fried green tomato, and try this Italian-inspired pasta recipe where the tomatoes are pureed into a vibrant and herb-packed sauce.

serves: 6 ~ *hands-on:* 26 min. ~ *total:* 26 min.

1 lb. uncooked spaghetti

¼ cup firmly packed fresh mint leaves

¼ cup firmly packed fresh basil leaves

¼ cup firmly packed arugula

¼ cup loosely packed fresh dill leaves

¾ tsp. kosher salt

¼ tsp. freshly ground black pepper

6 green tomatoes coarsely chopped

1 garlic clove

¼ cup extra virgin olive oil

4 oz. crumbled goat cheese

1. Cook pasta in boiling salted water in a Dutch oven according to package directions.

2. Meanwhile, process mint and next 7 ingredients in a food processor until minced. With processor running, pour oil through food chute; process until smooth.

3. Drain pasta, and return to Dutch oven. Add tomato mixture and goat cheese to pasta, stirring until cheese melts. Serve immediately.

MARKET TIP

Green tomatoes are great for cooking because they have a tart, bright flavor and hold up to grilling, pickling, or baking. Look for green tomatoes with firm, unblemished flesh.

Chapter
-3-
A NIBBLE
HERE
and There

Lima Bean Hummus... mmm!

Belle Veeta Dip

When you walk into a Southern home, you will invariably be greeted with two questions: "Can I get you anything to drink?" and "How about a little something to nibble on?" Both questions are entirely rhetorical. You'll be served despite any protestations you offer. In fact, the protest is part of the ritual—you're expected to briefly and politely decline before acquiescing. This tells your host that you are not so presumptuous as to expect food when you drop in, and you are so tempted by her culinary offerings that you simply cannot resist. This "dance of Southern hospitality," as I like to call it, includes another key component—the assurance of ease. Even as she chops, dices, and stirs, your host will assure you that the snacks she is hastily preparing are "not a bit of trouble." I was always taught that I should keep foodstuffs on hand and have a few tricks up my sleeve so I could quickly turn them into treats for unexpected guests. The ideal nibbles take something fresh from the garden and add a bit of sweetness or spice—just a simple touch to let guests know this food was prepared especially for them. Whatever the occasion, it's not the expense or difficulty of the recipe that counts. It's the message: Welcome!

Heirloom Tomato
BRUSCHETTA

Available in a rainbow of colors and varieties, heirloom tomatoes are easily found at local groceries—not just farmers' markets. Choose a mix of different hues to make a gorgeous presentation.

serves: 12 ~ *hands-on:* 8 min. ~ *total:* 8 min.

2 cups loosely packed fresh basil leaves, cut into thin strips

⅔ cup extra virgin olive oil

½ tsp. kosher salt

½ tsp. freshly ground black pepper

2 lb. assorted heirloom tomatoes, chopped or cut into half-moon–shaped slices

1 small red onion, quartered and thinly sliced

2 (12-oz.) French bread baguettes, halved horizontally

2 garlic cloves, peeled and halved

Garnish: small basil sprigs

1. Preheat broiler with oven rack 5 inches from heat. Combine first 6 ingredients in a large bowl.

2. Place baguette halves, cut sides up, on a baking sheet. Broil 1½ minutes or until toasted. Immediately rub cut sides of garlic over cut sides of baguette halves. Spoon tomato mixture over bread using a slotted spoon. Cut each baguette half crosswise into 6 pieces. Serve immediately.

MARKET TIP

You can tell if a tomato is ripe when you pick it up and it literally smells like a tomato. The unripe ones won't be fragrant, and the overripe ones will be soft.

Goat Cheese & Tapenade
TOASTS

These super-simple appetizers take only 10 minutes total. Whip these up, and you can get out of the kitchen quickly to mingle with your guests.

serves: 12 ~ *hands-on:* 10 min. ~ *total:* 10 min.

½ (12-oz.) *French bread baguette*

2 Tbsp. extra virgin olive oil, divided

½ tsp. fresh lemon juice (about ½ small lemon)

¼ tsp. freshly ground black pepper

1 (3-oz.) goat cheese log

½ cup organic black olive tapenade

2 Tbsp. coarsely chopped fresh oregano

1. Preheat oven to 450°. Cut baguette half in half lengthwise; brush cut sides with 2 tsp. oil. Place on a baking sheet, cut sides up. Bake at 450° for 5 minutes or until edges are golden.

2. Place lemon juice, pepper, goat cheese, and remaining 4 tsp. oil in a bowl; mash with a fork until blended. Spread cheese mixture on cut sides of baguette halves. Top with tapenade, and sprinkle with oregano. Cut each half into 6 pieces.

NOTE: We tested with Belle Chèvre goat cheese.

KITCHEN TIP

To add another flavorful element to these toasts, top them with quartered cherry tomatoes or sliced roasted red peppers.

Chicken Rillettes

RILLETTES

Rillettes is just a fancy French word for pulled meat that's combined with flavorful herbs, butter or lard, and a little cooking stock. They are traditionally served in little jars, which I find both adorable and convenient. You can make them with almost any meat. Check out my Pork Rillettes with Bourbon on page 131.

serves: 12 ~ *hands-on:* 26 min. ~ *total:* 4 hr., 36 min.

Chicken Rillettes

1 cup butter

1½ cups finely chopped shallots (about 6 shallots)

1 Tbsp. chopped fresh thyme

1 (2-lb.) whole deli-roasted chicken, skinned, boned, and finely shredded

2½ cups chicken stock

2 Tbsp. chopped fresh parsley

1 Tbsp. coarse-grained Dijon mustard

½ tsp. table salt

½ tsp. freshly ground black pepper

Crusty country bread or baguette slices

Pickles

1. Melt ¼ cup butter in large heavy skillet over medium heat. Add shallots; sauté 4 minutes or until tender. Add remaining ¾ cup butter to skillet; cook 2 minutes or until butter melts. Stir in thyme, chicken, and stock. Bring to a simmer; cook 10 minutes or until chicken is moist and tender and liquid is almost evaporated. Remove from heat, and cool 10 minutes. Stir in parsley and mustard. Sprinkle with salt and pepper.

2. Pack chicken mixture into 2 (8-oz.) jars. Cover and chill at least 4 hours.

3. Serve rillettes with crusty bread or baguette slices and pickles.

Sardine Rillettes

2 (4.38-oz.) cans sardines in oil, drained

1 lemon

⅓ cup finely chopped green onions (about 1 onion)

2 Tbsp. finely chopped celery

1 Tbsp. chopped fresh basil

2 Tbsp. goat cheese

¼ tsp. table salt

¼ tsp. freshly ground black pepper

12 (¼-inch-thick) diagonally cut French bread baguette slices, brushed with olive oil and toasted

1. Cut sardines in half lengthwise; remove and discard bones. Place sardine meat in a bowl; mash with a fork. Grate zest from lemon to equal ¼ tsp. Cut lemon in half; squeeze juice from half of lemon into a measuring spoon to equal 1 Tbsp. Reserve remaining lemon half for another use.

2. Add lemon juice, lemon zest, green onions, and next 5 ingredients to sardine meat; stir until blended. Cover and chill until ready to serve.

3. To serve, spoon sardine mixture evenly onto baguette slices.

Parmesan
CHEESE STRAWS

If you've never made cheese straws before, don't be intimidated…
I have a shortcut—puff pastry. This makes them supremely
light and crispy, plus it saves me the effort of preparing the
dough from scratch. I like to use Parmesan cheese instead of
the traditional Cheddar for a more delicate flavor.

serves: 8 ~ *hands-on:* 11 min. ~ *total:* 23 min.

1 large egg

½ cup (2 oz.) finely shredded Parmesan
   cheese

½ tsp. ground mustard

¼ tsp. table salt

⅛ tsp. ground red pepper

½ (17.3-oz.) package puff pastry sheets,
   thawed

Garnish: fresh thyme leaves

1. Preheat oven to 400°. Whisk together egg
and 1 Tbsp. water in a small bowl.

2. Combine cheese and next 3 ingredients in a
small bowl.

3. Roll dough into a 12-inch square on a lightly
floured surface. Cut dough in half crosswise;
brush both halves with egg wash. Sprinkle half
of dough with cheese mixture. Place remaining
half of dough on top of cheese mixture, egg
wash side down. Roll with a rolling pin to seal
sheets together.

4. Beginning with short side, cut dough crosswise
into 16 (about ¾-inch-wide) strips. Place strips,
1 inch apart, on 2 ungreased baking sheets. Twist
strips 3 times, stretching dough slightly and
pressing ends onto baking sheets to adhere.

5. Bake at 400° for 12 minutes or until puffed
and golden.

These appealing
appetizers make even
the simplest meals
feel special and worth
celebrating. I serve them
upright in a small vase
to show off the elegant
twist shapes and to entice
my guests to indulge.

Lima Bean HUMMUS

It may seem unexpected to use lima beans in hummus, but most any kind of bean can take the place of the traditional garbanzo. This recipe is the result of my "playing" in the kitchen, as I like to call it, and has since become one of my favorites.

makes: 3 cups ~ *hands-on:* 6 min. ~ *total:* 18 min.

1 (16-oz.) package frozen Fordhook lima beans

2 garlic cloves

2 tsp. kosher salt

½ tsp. freshly ground black pepper

⅛ tsp. ground red pepper

1 cup extra virgin olive oil

2 Tbsp. fresh lemon juice (about 1 lemon)

Pita bread rounds, cut into wedges

1. Cook lima beans in boiling water to cover 12 minutes or until very tender; drain.

2. With processor running, drop garlic through food chute; process until minced. Add lima beans, salt, and next 2 ingredients; process until smooth. With processor running, slowly add oil and lemon juice through food chute; process until blended. Serve with pita wedges.

KITCHEN TIP

A cup of olive oil may sound like a lot, but just add it slowly with the food processor running, and it blends perfectly.

"Belle-Veeta" DIP

I wasn't always an artisan cheesemaker, and I've never been a food snob—meaning that I have enjoyed "cheese-foods" (products that really aren't cheese at all but still, despite that fact, taste mighty good) like the ubiquitous Velveeta-and-Ro-Tel dip. I've found a way to make the same guilty delicious flavor using all the beauty and health benefits of "real" food!

makes: 3½ cups ~ *hands-on:* 15 min. ~ *total:* 15 min.

1 Tbsp. butter

½ tsp. annatto seeds

12 oz. goat cheese

1 (8-oz.) package cream cheese

1½ tsp. baking soda

1 (10-oz.) can diced tomatoes and green chiles, drained

Tortilla chips

1. Melt butter in a small saucepan over medium heat. Add annatto seeds; cook 30 seconds or until butter turns a deep orange color. Remove from heat. Pour butter through a fine wire-mesh strainer into a bowl; discard solids.

2. In same pan, combine goat cheese, cream cheese, and baking soda. Cook over medium heat until cheeses melt, stirring often. Stir in tomatoes and green chiles; add butter, and cook, stirring occasionally, 3-5 minutes or until thoroughly heated. Serve warm with tortilla chips.

When my son, Kelly, and I have a Saturday afternoon snack attack, we make some "Belle-Veeta" Dip for fun.

COCKTAIL
Party

SERVES 10

The Alabama Shake

The Gingerly

Spring Pea Crostini

Pork Rillettes with Bourbon

Cranberry-Pistachio Cheese Log

Refrigerator Pickled Vegetables

I'm all for hosting get-togethers that are simple yet impressive. A fun party is so easy to pull off with an appetizer spread of make-ahead recipes and a couple of specialty drinks. Let nature inspire your decorating—ferns make inexpensive fresh arrangements.

The Gingerly

The Alabama Shake

Cranberry-Pistachio Cheese Log

Refrigerator Pickled Vegetables

 ENTERTAINING TIP

Build an inviting appetizer spread:

- Arrange nibbles on large wooden boards
- Serve colorful pickled veggies and pork rillettes in mason jars with picks and spreaders
- Pile platters high with crackers and toasted breads, and tuck in crostini, cheeses, and fresh fruit

Spring Pea Crostini

Pork Rillettes with Bourbon

The Alabama Shake

serves: 1 ~ *hands-on:* 5 min.
total: 5 min.

¼ cup fresh lemon juice (about 2 lemons)

3 Tbsp. sugar

1½ Tbsp. bourbon

1⅓ cups brown ale

Garnish: fresh mint sprig

1. Combine first 3 ingredients in a cocktail shaker; fill shaker with ice. Cover with lid, and shake vigorously until sugar dissolves. Gently stir in ale. Strain into a chilled lemonade glass.

NOTE: We tested with Truck Stop Honey Brown Ale.

The Gingerly

serves: 10 ~ *hands-on:* 5 min.
total: 1 hr., 5 min.

½ cup sugar

2 tsp. fresh lemon juice (about ½ small lemon)

2 tsp. grated fresh ginger

1 (750-milliliter) bottle dry sparkling wine, chilled

10 lemon twists

1. Combine first 3 ingredients and ¼ cup water in a small saucepan. Bring to a boil, and boil 2 minutes or until syrupy. Pour mixture through a fine wire-mesh strainer into a small bowl, discarding solids. Cool completely (about 1 hour).

2. Pour 1 Tbsp. syrup into each of 10 tall glasses. Add ½ cup sparkling wine and 1 lemon twist to each glass. Stir gently.

Spring Pea Crostini

serves: 10 ~ *hands-on:* 8 min.
total: 8 min.

¼ cup chopped fresh mint

¼ cup olive oil

1 Tbsp. lemon juice (about 1 lemon)

½ tsp. table salt

¼ tsp. freshly ground black pepper

1 (16-oz.) package frozen English peas, thawed, or blanched fresh peas

1 bunch green onions, cut into 1-inch pieces

1 (12-oz.) French bread baguette, cut into 30 slices and toasted

2 oz. fresh Parmesan cheese, shaved

1. Process first 7 ingredients in a food processor 1 minute or until smooth, stopping to scrape down sides as needed.

2. Spread about 1½ Tbsp. pea mixture onto each toast. Top evenly with Parmesan cheese shavings.

Pork Rillettes with Bourbon

serves: 36 ~ hands-on: 21 min.
total: 12 hr., 16 min.

¼ cup chopped fresh thyme

2 Tbsp. sea salt

20 black peppercorns

6 juniper berries

4 bay leaves

2¾ lb. boneless pork shoulder (Boston butt), cut into 1-inch chunks

½ cup bourbon

1 cup lard, divided

2 cups chicken stock

2 Tbsp. chopped fresh parsley

36 (¼-inch-thick) diagonally-cut French bread baguette slices, toasted

Garnish: fresh parsley leaves, fresh thyme sprigs

1. Grind first 5 ingredients in a mortar bowl or spice grinder until coarse. Place pork in a large bowl. Add spice mixture and bourbon; toss well. Cover and marinate overnight.

2. Preheat oven to 225°. Melt 1 Tbsp. lard in a Dutch oven over medium heat. Drain pork, discarding marinade. Cook half of pork in hot lard, turning occasionally, 4-5 minutes or until browned on all sides; transfer to a plate with a slotted spoon. Brown remaining pork. Return pork to Dutch oven. Add remaining lard; cook over medium heat until lard melts. Stir in stock. Cover and bake at 225° for 3 hours or until pork is very tender.

3. Transfer pork to a large bowl using a slotted spoon, reserving cooking liquid. Shred pork. Stir ¼ cup cooking liquid and parsley into pork. Pack pork mixture into 6 (6-oz.) ramekins; press on surface of pork with the back of a spoon to achieve a flat surface. Cover and chill 30 minutes.

4. Let cooking liquid stand until fat separates. Skim 12 Tbsp. fat from top of liquid; reserve in a small bowl. Discard remaining cooking liquid. Spoon 2 Tbsp. reserved fat over each ramekin. Cover and chill until ready to serve. Serve pork mixture with toast slices.

KITCHEN TIP

By pouring the liquid fat over the pork and chilling it, you are sealing in the freshness and flavor. These will keep for up to 1 week with the fat layer intact and refrigerated.

Cranberry-Pistachio Cheese Log

serves: 12 ~ *hands-on:* 12 min.
total: 2 hr., 12 min.

8 oz. goat cheese, softened

8 oz. cream cheese, softened

½ cup sweetened dried cranberries, chopped

¾ tsp. orange zest

Parchment or wax paper

¾ cup shelled roasted, salted pistachios, coarsely chopped

Assorted crackers

1. Process goat cheese and cream cheese in a food processor until smooth. Transfer to a bowl. Stir in cranberries and orange zest.

2. Place cheese mixture on a large piece of parchment or wax paper. Using parchment, roll cheese mixture into a 9-inch log. Chill 2 hours or until firm.

3. Place pistachios on a sheet of parchment or wax paper. Gently roll cheese log in nuts to completely cover. Wrap log in another piece of parchment or wax paper; chill until ready to serve or up to 1 day. Serve with assorted crackers.

Refrigerator Pickled Vegetables

makes: 2 (1-pt. jars) ~ *hands-on:* 12 min. ~ *total:* 1 hr., 12 min., plus 1 day for marinating

½ tsp. mustard seeds

½ tsp. dried crushed red pepper

2 garlic cloves

2 (1-pt.) canning jars with lids

3 medium carrots, peeled

5 oz. fresh green beans, trimmed

5 oz. fresh okra

1 cup white vinegar

½ cup sugar

1 Tbsp. kosher salt

1. Place ¼ tsp. mustard seed, ¼ tsp. crushed red pepper, and 1 garlic clove in each of 2 (1-pt.) canning jars. Cut carrots in half crosswise; quarter lengthwise. Divide carrot, beans, and okra evenly between jars.

2. Bring vinegar, next 2 ingredients, and 1 cup water to a boil in a small saucepan, stirring to dissolve sugar and salt. Pour boiling brine over vegetables. Cover jars with lids, and cool completely (about 1 hour). Chill 24 hours before serving. Refrigerate in an airtight container up to 1 month.

DEVILED EGGS
with Goat Cheese & Pickled Okra

Deviled eggs conjure up memories for me of spring picnics and Sunday suppers, but for many, they are a holiday staple. Whenever you like to make them, try out this unique version with tangy pickled okra and creamy goat cheese.

serves: 7 ~ *hands-on:* 13 min. ~ *total:* 30 min.

7 large eggs

4 Tbsp. crumbled goat cheese, divided

1 Tbsp. fresh thyme leaves

2 Tbsp. mayonnaise

1 tsp. Dijon mustard

½ tsp. hot sauce

¼ tsp. table salt

¼ tsp. freshly ground black pepper

3 Tbsp. chopped pickled okra (about 3 pods)

1 Tbsp. fresh thyme leaves

1. Place eggs in a Dutch oven; add water to 1 inch above eggs. Bring to a boil; immediately remove from heat. Cover and let stand 12 minutes. Drain and return eggs to pan. Fill pan with cold water and ice; let stand 5 minutes or until eggs are thoroughly chilled.

2. Tap each egg firmly on the counter until cracks form all over the shell. Peel under cold running water. Cut eggs in half lengthwise. Remove yolks, and place in a small bowl. Arrange egg white halves on a serving tray.

3. Mash yolks with a fork; add 1 Tbsp. goat cheese and next 6 ingredients, mashing until smooth. Stir in okra. Spoon or pipe yolk mixture into egg white halves. Top with remaining 3 Tbsp. crumbled goat cheese and fresh thyme. Cover and chill until ready to serve.

There is a whole market out there of fancy plates made just for deviled eggs—porcelain, hand-painted, the works. But you don't need delicate serving dishes to make these look pretty; all you need is just a sprinkle of fresh thyme.

STUFFED PEPPERS
with Chèvre, Pecans & Golden Raisins

I grew up eating stuffed peppers at most of our family dinners. As it turns out, both sides of my family—the Greeks and the Southerners—made them, and their recipes weren't really that different. I make mine with golden raisins, pecans, and goat cheese, naturally.

makes: 1 dozen ~ *hands-on:* 21 min. ~ *total:* 49 min.

12 sweet mini peppers

¼ tsp. table salt

¼ tsp. freshly ground black pepper

4 oz. goat cheese, softened

¼ cup pecan halves, toasted and chopped

¼ cup thinly sliced fresh basil, divided

¼ cup golden raisins, divided

1 Tbsp. olive oil

Garnish: small fresh basil leaves

1. Preheat broiler. Broil peppers on an aluminum foil-lined baking sheet 5 inches from heat, turning occasionally, 8 minutes or until peppers look blackened.

2. Place peppers in a large zip-top plastic freezer bag; seal and let stand 10 minutes to loosen skins. Reduce oven temperature to 450°.

3. Peel peppers. Make a slit in one side of each pepper; sprinkle with salt and black pepper.

4. Stir together cheese, pecans, 2 Tbsp. basil, and 2 Tbsp. raisins in a small bowl. Spoon cheese mixture evenly into peppers, pressing gently to close slits.

5. Return peppers to baking sheet, and drizzle with oil. Bake at 450° for 10 minutes or until cheese is bubbly.

6. Arrange peppers on a serving plate; sprinkle with remaining 2 Tbsp. basil and remaining 2 Tbsp. raisins.

MARKET TIP

Look for the small, sweet mini peppers in the produce section of the grocery store. These aren't spicy like jalapeños or large like bell peppers.

Fried Green TOMATOES

At the end of summer, as the air begins to cool, green tomatoes will be very plentiful, and red juicy tomatoes harder and harder to find. Take advantage of this bounty by frying the firm green ones in a crispy panko coating. No need for sauce or dip—they're wonderful on their own.

serves: 5 ~ hands-on: 16 min. ~ total: 16 min.

Canola oil

1½ cups all-purpose flour

¼ tsp. freshly ground black pepper

¼ tsp. paprika

¼ tsp. ground red pepper

1¼ tsp. kosher salt, divided

2 large eggs

2 cups panko (Japanese breadcrumbs)

2 medium-size green tomatoes, each cut into 5 (¼-inch-thick) slices

1. Pour oil to depth of 1 inch into a 6-qt. Dutch oven; heat to 350°.

2. Whisk together flour, next 3 ingredients, and 1 tsp. salt in a shallow dish. Whisk eggs in a medium bowl. Place panko in another shallow dish.

3. Sprinkle tomato slices with remaining ¼ tsp. salt; dredge in flour mixture. Dip in egg, and dredge in panko. Fry tomato slices, in batches, 2 minutes on each side or until golden brown. Drain on paper towels. Serve immediately.

⌒⌒ KITCHEN TIP ⌒⌒

When frying green tomatoes, don't flip them more than once or move them around in the pan unnecessarily so the breading stays intact.

Okra FRITTERS

These fritters are different from standard fried okra, which is generally covered in a cornmeal dusting and fried. This okra is sliced lengthwise, battered, and fried, resulting in a crunchy coating perfect for dunking in some homemade Ranch dressing.

serves: 6-8 ~ *hands-on:* 13 min. ~ *total:* 13 min.

½ cup all-purpose flour

½ tsp. table salt

½ tsp. freshly ground black pepper

½ cup chopped green onions

½ cup heavy cream

1 large egg

½ lb. fresh okra, trimmed and cut in half lengthwise

Vegetable oil

Ranch Dressing (page 67)

1. Whisk together first 3 ingredients in a medium bowl. Add green onions; toss to coat.

2. Whisk together cream and egg in a small bowl; add to dry mixture, stirring just until moistened. Fold in okra.

3. Pour oil to depth of 2 inches into a 6-qt. Dutch oven; heat over medium-high heat to 350°. Drop okra pieces one by one into hot oil. Fry in 3 batches, turning once, 5 minutes or until golden. Drain on a wire rack over paper towels. Serve immediately with Ranch Dressing.

MARKET TIP

Select smaller, more tender okra pods (less than 4 inches long) that are firm, brightly colored, and free of blemishes.

Zucchini FRIES

Yellow summer squash, golden zucchini, and common green zucchini all work well in this recipe, so use whichever you have on hand, or whichever is growing in your garden. I love to serve this with a garlic-y mayonnaise dip spiked with a little Creole mustard.

serves: 4-6 ~ *hands-on:* 12 min. ~ *total:* 32 min.

1 lb. zucchini (2 medium)

1 tsp. kosher salt, divided

1 cup panko (Japanese breadcrumbs)

¼ tsp. garlic powder

¼ tsp. freshly ground black pepper

1 cup all-purpose flour

2 large eggs

Vegetable oil

Southern Aïoli

1. Cut zucchini into 2- x ¼-inch sticks. Sprinkle sticks with ½ tsp. salt. Let stand 20 minutes. Rinse; drain and pat dry with paper towels.

2. Combine panko, garlic powder, and pepper in a medium bowl; place flour in a separate medium bowl. Whisk eggs in a small bowl.

3. Dredge zucchini sticks in flour; shake off excess. Dip zucchini sticks in eggs, and dredge in panko mixture.

4. Pour oil to depth of ¼ inch into a large skillet. Heat over medium-high heat until oil is hot and shimmers. Fry zucchini in 2 batches, turning after 1 minute, 2 minutes or until golden. Transfer to a paper towel–lined plate, and sprinkle with remaining ½ tsp. salt. Serve immediately with Southern Aïoli.

Southern Aïoli

makes: 1 cup ~ *hands-on:* 5 min.
total: 1 hr., 5 min.

1 cup mayonnaise

1 Tbsp. minced garlic (2 garlic cloves)

1 Tbsp. Creole mustard

2 tsp. fresh lemon juice (about ½ small lemon)

⅛ tsp. table salt

1. Combine all ingredients in a small bowl. Cover and chill at least 1 hour before serving.

LENTIL CAKES
with Squash Confetti

I love to use ingredients in unexpected ways, like the lentils in these little cakes. One is perfect as an appetizer for a dinner party; two or three work well as a main course with a salad.

serves: 8 ~ *hands-on:* 26 min. ~ *total:* 26 min.

6 Tbsp. olive oil, divided

¾ cup chopped onion

¼ cup chopped carrot

1 garlic clove, chopped

1 (15-oz.) can lentils, drained

1 large egg, beaten

1 cup fine, dry breadcrumbs, divided

½ tsp. table salt, divided

½ tsp. freshly ground black pepper, divided

1 large egg, beaten

¼ cup all-purpose flour

½ (1½-lb.) butternut squash, peeled and diced (about 2 cups)

8 tsp. sour cream

2 Tbsp. chopped fresh chives

1. Heat 1 Tbsp. oil in a large skillet over medium-high heat. Add onion, carrot, and garlic; sauté 3 minutes or until onion is tender. Combine onion mixture, lentils, 1 egg, ¼ cup breadcrumbs, ¼ tsp. salt, and ¼ tsp. pepper in a bowl. Shape lentil mixture into 8 (¾-inch-thick) patties.

2. Heat ¼ cup oil in a large skillet over medium-high heat. Whisk together 1 egg and 2 Tbsp. water in a small bowl. Place flour in a shallow bowl. Place remaining ¾ cup breadcrumbs in another shallow bowl. Dredge patties in flour; dip in egg mixture, and dredge in breadcrumbs. Fry patties in hot oil 2 minutes on each side or until golden. Drain on paper towels.

3. Heat remaining 1 Tbsp. oil in same large skillet over medium-high heat. Add squash, and sauté 5 minutes or until tender and golden. Sprinkle with remaining ¼ tsp. salt and remaining ¼ tsp. pepper.

4. Dollop 1 tsp. sour cream onto each lentil cake. Top lentil cakes with squash; sprinkle with chives.

Sweet Potato
CAKES

Potato cakes are easy to make and create the perfect side for roasted or grilled meats. You can top these with endless options, including crème fraîche, sour cream, chutney, pepper jelly, and salsa. My favorite topping is Hot Bengal chutney, which is basically spicy fruit and tomato preserves.

serves: 5 ~ *hands-on:* 10 min. ~ *total:* 22 min.

3 Tbsp. grated onion

1 (8-oz.) sweet potato, peeled and coarsely grated

1 (8-oz.) baking potato, peeled and coarsely grated

2 large eggs, beaten

1 Tbsp. all-purpose flour

2 Tbsp. finely chopped fresh cilantro

1 tsp. kosher salt

1 tsp. ground cumin

1 tsp. garam masala

1 garlic clove, minced

½ cup canola oil

Hot Bengal chutney

Sour cream

Garnish: fresh cilantro leaves

1. Preheat oven to 300°. Place first 3 ingredients in a kitchen towel or several layers of paper towels; squeeze to remove excess liquid. Place vegetables in a large bowl. Stir in eggs and next 6 ingredients.

2. Heat oil in large heavy skillet over medium-high heat.

3. Scoop potato mixture by ¼ cupfuls, and shape into 10 (2-inch) patties; flatten slightly. Fry patties, in 2 batches, in hot oil 3 minutes on each side or until golden. Drain on a wire rack over paper towels. Serve with chutney and sour cream.

For me, the ideal nibbles take something fresh from the garden and add a bit of sweetness or spice—just a simple touch to let guests know this food was prepared especially for them.

Deep-Fried OYSTERS

I believe that it's not really summer until I've set foot on a beach. Living in North Alabama, it's a pretty long drive all the way down to the coast, but always worth the effort. As soon as we arrive, we hunt down our favorite dive for fried oysters or oysters on the half shell. If I can't get to the shore, I make them at home. This easy buttermilk-cornmeal coating gets a kick from Cajun seasoning.

serves: 6-8 ~ *hands-on:* 15 min. ~ *total:* 15 min.

1 cup mayonnaise

¼ cup Asian hot chili sauce (such as Sriracha)

Peanut oil

1 pt. fresh standard oysters, drained

1 cup buttermilk

2 cups plain yellow cornmeal

1 Tbsp. Cajun seasoning

1 tsp. table salt

1. Stir together mayonnaise and hot chili sauce in a small bowl until blended.

2. Pour oil to depth of 1½ inches into a 4-qt. saucepan; heat to 375°. Combine oysters and buttermilk in a medium bowl.

3. Whisk together cornmeal, Cajun seasoning, and salt in a shallow dish. Drain oysters well. Dredge oysters, 1 at a time, in cornmeal mixture, shaking off excess; place on a baking sheet.

4. Fry oysters, in 6 batches, 30 seconds to 1 minute or until golden and crisp. Remove oysters from oil using a slotted spoon, and drain on a wire rack over paper towels. Serve immediately with mayonnaise mixture.

KITCHEN TIP

If you're making a big batch of these, keep them warm in a 200° oven while you fry the rest.

Corn & Crab FRITTERS

I love crab cakes, but they can be pretty fussy to make. The more crab you put in, the more fragile they become. So I started making these crab fritters instead. They are much easier to prepare, and they look great piled up in a paper towel-lined basket or in paper cones like French fries.

makes: about 3 dozen ~ *hands-on:* 31 min. ~ *total:* 46 min.

1 lb. fresh lump crabmeat, drained

1 Tbsp. butter

1¼ cups fresh corn kernels (2 ears)

1 small onion, finely chopped

1 cup all-purpose flour

1 tsp. baking powder

½ tsp. freshly ground black pepper

⅛ tsp. dried crushed red pepper

1 tsp. table salt, divided

⅔ cup milk

2 large eggs

⅓ cup chopped fresh cilantro

Vegetable oil

1 cup mayonnaise

1 Tbsp. chopped fresh cilantro

1½ Tbsp. fresh lime juice (about 2 limes)

2 tsp. Asian hot chili sauce (such as Sriracha)

1. Pick crabmeat, removing any bits of shell. Melt butter in a medium skillet over medium heat. Add corn and onion; cook, stirring occasionally, 8 minutes or until onion is tender. Remove from heat, and cool 5 minutes.

2. Combine flour, next 3 ingredients, and ½ tsp. salt in a large bowl. Whisk together milk and eggs in a medium bowl. Gradually whisk milk mixture into flour mixture until smooth. Stir in corn mixture, crabmeat, and ⅓ cup cilantro. Cover and chill 10 minutes.

3. Preheat oven to 250°. Pour oil to depth of ¼ inch into a large skillet; heat over medium-high heat. Fry batter by tablespoonfuls, in 5 batches, in hot oil 1 minute on each side or until golden brown. Drain on a wire rack; keep warm at 250° until all batches are cooked.

4. Whisk together mayonnaise, next 3 ingredients, and remaining ½ tsp. salt in a bowl. Serve mayonnaise mixture with fritters.

HIGHBROW PIGS
in a Shawl

I've always loved pigs in a blanket, but I knew they could be even better with just a couple tweaks. Instead of crescent dough, I use puff pastry. I also roll them up and slice them in rounds before baking, so they look like savory cookies.

makes: 2 dozen ~ *hands-on:* 8 min. ~ *total:* 48 min.

1 large egg yolk

½ (17.3-oz) package frozen puff pastry sheets, thawed and cut into 4 rectangles

4 (3-oz.) andouille sausages

Butter

Pepper jelly

1. Preheat oven to 375°. Whisk together egg yolk and 1 Tbsp. water in a small bowl. Brush 1 long side of each pastry rectangle with egg mixture. Place 1 sausage along opposite side of each rectangle; roll up, pressing edges to seal. Place in freezer for 15 minutes or until dough is slightly firm.

2. Cut each log crosswise into 6 equal slices. Place 1 slice, cut side down, in each of 24 buttered muffin cups. Bake at 375° for 25 minutes or until pastry is golden and sausage sizzles. Drain on paper towels. Serve with jelly.

Sausage & Sweet Potato
HAND PIES

Just about every cuisine has some version of hand pies or fried pies—both sweet and savory. I'm always trying out different flavor combinations with mine, but I find myself leaning toward the savory ones. A little heavy cream balances out the strong spices of coriander and cumin that flavor the sweet potato filling.

serves: 12 ~ *hands-on:* 10 min. ~ *total:* 1 hr., 50 min.

1 large sweet potato

¼ cup heavy cream

⅛ tsp. kosher salt

⅛ tsp. ground coriander

⅛ tsp. ground cumin

⅛ tsp. freshly ground black pepper

3 patties Garlic & Sage Breakfast Sausage (page 46), cooked and crumbled

1 cup frozen sweet peas

1 (17.3-oz.) package frozen puff pastry sheets, thawed

1 large egg, lightly beaten

Parchment paper

1. Preheat oven to 400°. Place sweet potato on a baking sheet. Bake at 400° for 1 hour. Let stand 15 minutes or until cool enough to handle.

2. Peel sweet potato, and mash with a potato masher to measure 1½ cups. Stir together sweet potato, cream, and next 6 ingredients in a medium bowl.

3. Roll each pastry sheet into a 12-inch square on a lightly floured surface; cut each square into 6 (6- x 4-inch) rectangles. Spoon ¼ cup filling into center of each square. Moisten edges of rectangles with a brush dipped in beaten egg. Fold 1 corner of each rectangle over filling onto opposite corner, stretching and pressing edges together with a fork to seal into a triangular shape. Cut slits in triangles to vent. Brush with remaining egg. Place triangles on a baking sheet lined with parchment paper.

4. Bake at 400° for 25 minutes or until golden and crisp. Serve warm.

I ♥ bourbon!

Mint Julep

Bellini Shiners

Chapter
-4-

SIPS, SHAKES,
and Shines

In my native Alabama, we place a premium on liquid refreshment. Maybe that's because the same mercury that rises above 90 in summertime can dip below freezing in winter. And when you're "just about to burn up" or "freezing half to death," nothing cools you down or warms you up like a great beverage.

And I think what draws us to special drinks is the way they can turn an impromptu gathering into an occasion. Take a platter of simple appetizers, add just one special drink served in festive glasses, and you've got a party. Some drinks are such a part of our culture that we can't imagine marking an occasion without them. What would Derby Day be without mint juleps or Cinco de Mayo without margaritas, perhaps with pomegranate? Fresh ingredients are the key to great cocktails for the grown-ups, as well as special treats for the kids. It's so easy to find ripe, juicy berries for Homemade Strawberry Milk, and that fresh fruit takes a good-for-you drink and instantly makes it fun and special. I love plucking the purply-black blackberries fresh from the vine, perfect for making Blackberry-Cucumber Sweet Tea.

On hot summer days and chilly winter evenings, at gatherings large and small, add a few of my favorite drinks to your menu. Cheers!

Pomegranate
MARGARITAS

This recipe is a great way to enliven the classic margarita. The flavor profile is bold but not overpowering, and the vibrant ruby color is the perfect addition to any party.

*serves: 2 ~ **hands-on:** 3 min. ~ **total:** 3 min.*

Margarita salt

Lime wedge

½ cup white tequila

½ cup pomegranate juice

¼ cup orange liqueur

1 Tbsp. fresh lime juice (about 1 lime)

Garnishes: lime wedges, mint sprigs

1. Pour margarita salt onto a plate or shallow dish. Run lime wedge along rim of 2 margarita glasses; dip rims of glasses into salt. Fill glasses with ice.

2. Fill a cocktail shaker with ice; add tequila and next 3 ingredients. Cover with lid, and shake vigorously until thoroughly chilled (about 30 seconds). Strain into prepared glasses. Serve immediately.

NOTE: We tested with Triple Sec orange liqueur.

KITCHEN TIP

Make this drink your own by substituting other fruit juices, such as grapefruit or tangerine, or even peach nectar, for the pomegranate.

Spiked Jalapeño
LEMONADE

I've always been a fan of homemade lemonade—the perfect balance of sweet and tart served super cold in a tall glass with ice. But this variation takes lemonade up a notch! Fresh jalapeños, tequila, and a martini shaker turn a roadside-stand classic into a party-ready adult refresher.

serves: 1 ~ *hands-on:* 5 min. ~ *total:* 5 min.

3 Tbsp. tequila

1½ Tbsp. fresh lemon juice (about 1 lemon)

1½ Tbsp. Simple Syrup (page 169)

1 drop vanilla extract

1 jalapeño pepper slice

Garnishes: jalapeño pepper slices, lemon twist

1. Combine first 5 ingredients in a cocktail shaker; fill shaker with ice. Cover with lid, and shake vigorously until thoroughly chilled (about 20 seconds). Strain into a chilled martini glass. Serve immediately.

KITCHEN TIP

When working with hot peppers, be sure to wear gloves. The capsaicin can burn your fingers (or eyes) if you get it on you.

Rum
CHILLER

Cool down with my take on an iced coffee. A bit of lime brings together this unexpected combination of rum and coffee.

serves: 1 ~ ***hands-on:*** 5 min. ~ ***total:*** 5 min.

¼ *cup rum*

2 Tbsp. cold strong-brewed coffee

1 Tbsp. Simple Syrup (page 169)

Fresh lime wedge or lime twist

1. Combine first 3 ingredients in an ice-filled cocktail shaker. Cover with lid, and shake vigorously. Strain into a double old-fashioned glass filled with ice. Squeeze juice from lime wedge into cocktail; add squeezed wedge to cocktail.

When I entertain, a specialty drink never fails to liven up the party or turn an impromptu gathering into an occasion.

Ginger
MINT JULEP

It's pretty well known that a mint julep is synonymous with Derby Day, but did you know that it's also one of the oldest cocktails in America? I think any classic recipe deserves a fresh update, so I make my juleps with homemade ginger syrup.

serves: 1 ~ *hands-on:* 5 min. ~ *total:* 45 min.

1 Tbsp. Ginger Syrup (page 240)

6 fresh mint leaves

⅓ cup bourbon

1 cup crushed ice

Garnishes: Candied Ginger (page 240), mint sprigs

1. Muddle Ginger Syrup and mint in a mint julep cup to release flavors. Add bourbon and crushed ice; stir until outside of cup is frosted.

⤳ KITCHEN TIP ⤳

Crushed ice is critical in a julep.
Crush cubes in a plastic bag with a mallet
or use your food processor.

Blackberry
BLOSSOM

If you've ever lived near a wooded area, you've hopefully experienced the joy of stumbling upon wild blackberries. My childhood was jam-packed with afternoons spent gathering them and eating just about as many as I brought home. Nowadays, I make this cocktail on sultry summer nights, and all of those juicy memories come rushing back to me.

serves: 1 ~ *hands-on:* 6 min. ~ *total:* 6 min.

6 blackberries

2 Tbsp. apple brandy

2 Tbsp. bourbon

1½ Tbsp. fresh lemon juice (about 1 lemon)

1½ Tbsp. Simple Syrup

Crushed ice

Garnish: 1 blackberry

1. Muddle 6 blackberries in a cocktail shaker to release flavors; add brandy and next 3 ingredients. Fill shaker with ice; cover with lid, and shake vigorously until thoroughly chilled (about 30 seconds). Strain into a double old-fashioned glass filled with crushed ice.

Simple Syrup

makes: about ¾ cup ~ *hands-on:* 1 min.
total: 2 min.

½ cup sugar

1. Place sugar in a 2-cup glass measuring cup; stir in ½ cup water. Microwave at HIGH 1 minute; stir mixture until sugar dissolves. Refrigerate in an airtight container.

Even now, whenever I discover blackberries along my hiking path or along a country road, I pick a few for a deliciously spontaneous snack.

Bourbon
ICED TEA

Everyone has their own swear-by-it recipe for sweet tea, using lemons or lemonade, buckets of sugar, and even oranges and limes. When I make tea, I make it for a party— bourbon-laced and sweetened with the most flavorful honey I can find. Try this recipe at home for your own signature drink.

serves: 5 ~ *hands-on:* 7 min. ~ *total:* 3 hr., 14 min.

4 cups boiling water

8 regular-size tea bags

1 cup honey-flavored bourbon

¼ cup honey

Garnishes: lemon slices, mint sprigs

1. Pour boiling water over tea bags; cover and steep 7 minutes.

2. Remove and discard tea bags. Cover and chill 3 hours.

3. Stir in bourbon and honey. Serve over ice.

NOTE: *We tested with Jack Daniel's Tennessee Honey.*

KITCHEN TIP

For perfectly brewed tea, follow these simple rules:
Don't let it steep too long, don't squeeze the tea bags,
and keep the pitcher covered.

Tasia's
SAZERAC

I love to take a classic drink and give it my own spin, even if it's just a couple ever-so-slight improvements. I've upgraded from plain simple syrup to a honey-flavored one, and with all the incredible varieties of bitters available today, I couldn't help but try out lemon bitters. Then, I use the best rye whiskey I can find for this cocktail; my personal favorite is Pappy Van Winkle Rye.

serves: 2 ~ *hands-on:* 5 min. ~ *total:* 7 min.

½ cup rye whiskey

1 Tbsp. Honey Syrup

¾ tsp. lemon bitters

2 tsp. absinthe

2 lemon peel strips

1. Fill 3 rocks glasses with ice; set 2 glasses aside to chill.

2. Combine first 3 ingredients in an ice-filled cocktail shaker or third rocks glass; stir until thoroughly chilled.

3. Discard ice from reserved 2 glasses; add 1 tsp. absinthe to each, swirling to coat bottom and sides of glasses. Pour off and discard excess absinthe from each glass.

4. Strain whiskey mixture evenly into absinthe-coated glasses. For each drink: twist 1 lemon peel strip over drink to release citrus oils, rub peel around rim of glass, and add to drink.

Honey Syrup

makes: about ⅔ cup ~ *hands-on:* 1 min.
total: 2 min.

½ cup honey

1. Combine honey and ¼ cup water in a 2-cup glass measuring cup. Microwave at HIGH 45 seconds or until warm; stir until honey dissolves. Refrigerate in an airtight container.

Peach
MOONSHINE

I made this for a farm party one summer, and it was such a hit! I try to let the seasons inspire a special twist to an otherwise basic drink. In this case, it's the perfectly ripe peaches of Chilton County, Alabama.

makes: 3 (1-qt.) jars ~ *hands-on:* 11 min. ~ *total:* 21 min.

3 (1-qt.) canning jars

3 lemon thyme sprigs

¾ cup sugar

6 peaches, peeled, pitted, and quartered

3 (750-milliliter) bottles white corn whiskey (about 9 cups)

1. Place jars and lids in a large stockpot with water to cover. Bring to a boil; reduce heat, and simmer 10 minutes.

2. Remove jars from water. Place 1 lemon thyme sprig, ¼ cup sugar, and 8 peach quarters in each jar. Carefully pour about 3 cups whiskey into each jar, leaving ¼-inch headspace.

3. Wipe jar rims. Cover at once with metal lids, and screw on bands. Turn jars upside down and then right side up several times to dissolve sugar. Store in a cool place for 3 weeks.

NOTE: We tested with Prichard's Lincoln County Lightning for the white corn whiskey.

MARKET TIP

Look for fruit that is firm with taut, unblemished skin and no signs of bruising or wrinkles. If you smell peaches when you walk up to the stand, you know they are ripe.

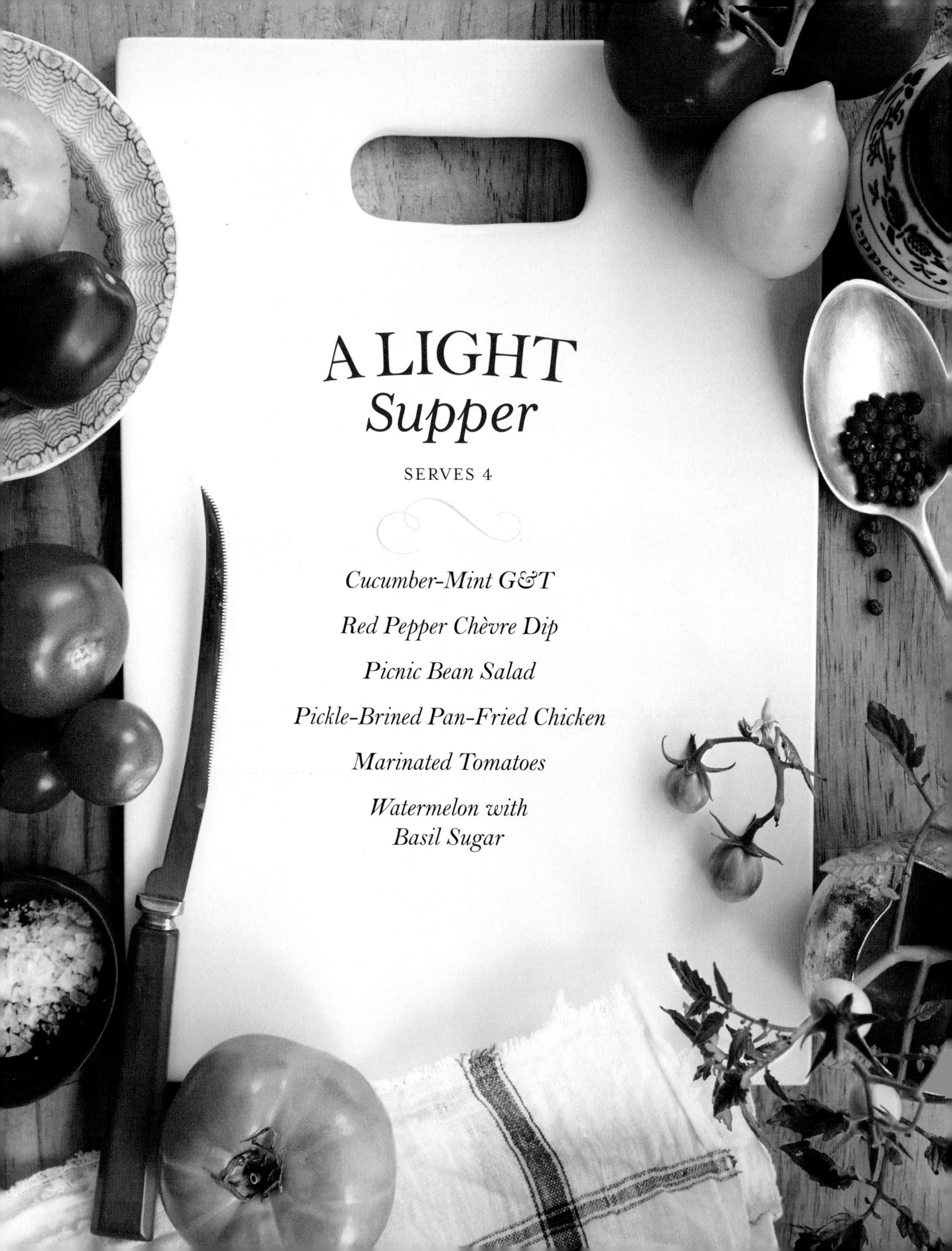

A LIGHT
Supper

SERVES 4

Cucumber-Mint G&T

Red Pepper Chèvre Dip

Picnic Bean Salad

Pickle-Brined Pan-Fried Chicken

Marinated Tomatoes

Watermelon with
Basil Sugar

When summer produce is at the peak of perfection, this menu showcases it in all its vivid glory. There's nothing better than serving these seasonal gems outside under the setting sun amidst a soft evening breeze. If I could, I'd serve every meal alfresco.

Picnic Bean Salad

Cucumber-Mint G&T

Red Pepper Chèvre Dip

Pickle-Brined Pan-Fried Chicken

∽ ENTERTAINING TIP ∼

To create your own floral arrangements:

- Let one color, such as white or yellow, guide your flower choices
- Take advantage of blossoming branches and shrubs from your own garden
- Add touches of green with hydrangea or fig leaves
- Group arrangements of all sizes—even single blooms

Marinated Tomatoes

Watermelon with Basil Sugar

Cucumber–Mint G&T

Cucumber is so refreshing. Coupled with mint in this Gin & Tonic, it is sure to please. This combination, sans gin, is a lovely water that will make you feel like a guest at a luxury spa.

serves: 1 ~ *hands-on:* 5 min.
total: 5 min.

4 fresh mint leaves

4 thin English cucumber slices

¼ cup gin

Tonic water

1. Muddle mint and cucumber in a highball glass to release flavors.

2. Fill glass with ice; top with gin. Add tonic water, and stir gently.

Red Pepper Chèvre Dip

makes: 2½ cups ~ *hands-on:* 7 min.
total: 7 min.

11 oz. goat cheese, softened

¾ tsp. paprika

¼ tsp. ground red pepper

1 (12-oz.) jar roasted red bell peppers, drained, rinsed, and coarsely chopped

Toasted pita wedges

1. Beat first 4 ingredients at medium speed with an electric mixer until blended. Serve with pita wedges.

Picnic Bean Salad

Bean salad may conjure up images of old-fashioned church picnics; while that is a favorable image, this salad is an updated and enhanced version that will change its old reputation.

serves: 6 ~ *hands-on:* 11 min.
total: 26 min.

1 cup sugar snap peas

¼ cup extra virgin olive oil

3 Tbsp. chopped fresh basil

2 Tbsp. chopped fresh mint

1 Tbsp. chopped shallots

½ tsp. kosher salt

½ tsp. lemon zest

½ tsp. honey

1 Tbsp. fresh lemon juice (about 1 lemon)

¼ tsp. freshly ground black pepper

5 large radishes, thinly sliced

1 (16-oz.) can navy beans, drained and rinsed

1. Cook peas in boiling water to cover 30 seconds; drain. Plunge peas into ice water to stop the cooking process; drain. Cut peas in half crosswise.

2. Whisk together oil and next 8 ingredients in a large bowl. Add peas, radishes, and beans; toss well. Let stand, stirring occasionally, 15 minutes.

Pickle-Brined Pan-Fried Chicken

This chicken recipe will resemble your favorite Southern chicken sandwich. The surprise ingredient is pickle juice! It makes for tender and juicy pieces of chicken, and the panko breading gives them a great crunch.

serves: 4 ~ *hands-on:* 24 min.
total: 8 hr., 24 min.

4 skinned and boned chicken breasts (about 1¾ lb.)

2 cups dill pickle juice

¼ cup all-purpose flour

2 tsp. kosher salt

½ tsp. freshly ground black pepper

2 cups panko (Japanese breadcrumbs)

2 large eggs

Canola oil

Garnish: lemon wedges

1. Place chicken between 2 sheets of heavy-duty plastic wrap, and flatten to ¼-inch thickness using a flat side of a meat mallet or rolling pin. Place chicken in a large zip-top plastic freezer bag. Add pickle juice to bag; seal bag, and turn to coat. Chill 8 hours.

2. Remove chicken from pickle juice, discarding pickle juice. Pat chicken dry with paper towels.

3. Preheat oven to 200°. Whisk together flour, 1 tsp. salt, and pepper in a shallow dish. Whisk together panko and remaining 1 tsp. salt in another shallow dish. Whisk eggs in a medium bowl.

4. Dredge chicken in flour mixture; shake off excess. Dip in egg; dredge in panko mixture, patting firmly to adhere. Place chicken on a piece of plastic wrap.

5. Pour oil to depth of ¼ inch into a large skillet; heat over medium-high heat. Fry chicken, in batches, 3 minutes on each side or until golden brown and desired degree of doneness. Transfer chicken to a wire rack set in a jelly-roll pan. Keep warm in oven at 200° until ready to serve. Place chicken on a serving platter.

For a simple but satisfying weeknight meal, I serve Pickle-Brined Pan-Fried Chicken with an arugula salad and a few wedges of lemon.

Marinated Tomatoes

These tomatoes make a perfect side dish for any summer meal. The longer they steep, the better they taste. They are best served at room temperature.

serves: 8-10 ~ *hands-on:* 15 min.
total: 2 hr., 15 min.

¾ *cup olive oil*

½ *cup red wine vinegar*

¼ *cup chopped fresh basil*

1 Tbsp. sugar

1½ tsp. kosher salt

½ *tsp. freshly ground black pepper*

½ *tsp. chopped fresh thyme*

3 green onions, chopped

2 garlic cloves, minced

6 large tomatoes (3¼ lb.), each cut into 8 wedges

1. Whisk together all ingredients, except tomatoes, in a large bowl. Add tomatoes, tossing gently to coat. Cover and chill 2 hours.

Watermelon with Basil Sugar

Not that Mother Nature needs much help with her delicious creation of watermelon, but I just can't help dressing this fresh treat with a sprinkling of fresh basil sugar.

serves: 4 ~ *hands-on:* 5 min.
total: 5 min.

½ *cup sugar*

⅓ *cup coarsely chopped fresh basil*

8 (1-inch-thick) triangular-shaped seedless watermelon wedges

1. Process sugar and basil in a food processor until blended. Stand up watermelon wedges on rind ends on a platter. Sprinkle with basil sugar. Serve immediately.

Rummy Strawberry–Rhubarb
PUNCH

When rhubarb is in season, you can't miss it. Bunches of scarlet-hued stalks will practically jump off the produce shelves and into your grocery cart. Normally, I just make a pie or galette with this tart fruit, but sometimes I like to get creative, pairing it with its best friend, the strawberry, and turning it into a bubbly cocktail.

serves: 11 ~ *hands-on:* 7 min. ~ *total:* 1 hr., 13 min.

2 cups sliced fresh strawberries

½ cup honey

⅓ cup fresh orange juice (about 1 orange)

3½ cups coarsely chopped rhubarb (about 1 lb.)

1 cup rum

1 (750-milliliter) bottle Prosecco

Garnishes: Candied Rhubarb, fresh strawberries

1. Combine first 4 ingredients and ¼ cup water in a medium saucepan. Bring to a boil; reduce heat, and simmer 6 minutes.

2. Pour mixture through a wire-mesh strainer into a bowl. (Do not press solids.) Cool completely (about 1 hour). Cover and store in refrigerator.

3. Combine syrup, rum, and Prosecco in a large punch bowl.

Candied Rhubarb

makes: 1 cup ~ *hands-on:* 5 min.
total: 45 min.

1 (11-inch) rhubarb stalk

2 cups sugar

1. Cut rhubarb in half lengthwise. Cut crosswise into ¾-inch pieces.

2. Place 1 cup sugar in a shallow dish. Combine 1 cup water and remaining 1 cup sugar in a saucepan; bring to a boil over high heat. Boil 5 minutes, stirring until sugar dissolves. Add rhubarb, and boil 2 minutes. Using a slotted spoon, add rhubarb to sugar in shallow dish. Toss rhubarb in sugar to coat; using a slotted spoon, transfer to a wire rack or baking sheet, shaking off excess sugar. Cool completely (about 30 minutes).

Bellini
SHINERS

I find traditional bellinis a little bit boring. Why not add some fresh basil or kick it up a little with homemade peach moonshine? Basil brings out the summery aroma of peaches; it's like walking through a peach orchard and picking them yourself.

serves: 10 ~ *hands-on:* 5 min. ~ *total:* 5 min.

20 fresh basil leaves

5 fresh peach slices

5 Tbsp. powdered sugar

1¼ cups sparkling water

15 Tbsp. Peach Moonshine (page 174)

2½ Tbsp. fresh lime juice (about 2 limes)

1 (750-milliliter) bottle Prosecco

Garnishes: torn basil leaves, fresh peach slices

1. For every 2 servings, muddle 4 basil leaves, 1 peach slice, and 1 Tbsp. powdered sugar in a cocktail shaker to release flavors. Add ½ cup ice. Add ¼ cup sparkling water, 3 Tbsp. Peach Moonshine, and 1½ tsp. lime juice. Cover with lid, and shake vigorously until thoroughly chilled (about 30 seconds). Strain evenly into 2 chilled Champagne flutes. Top each serving with ⅓ cup Prosecco. Serve immediately.

MARKET TIP

If you don't have time to make the Peach Moonshine yourself, many liquor stores now carry fruit-flavored moonshines like peach.

Pool Party Watermelon
PUNCH

What says summer more than a big ruby watermelon? Usually, I'm a little overly ambitious when buying one at the store, and then I'm left trying to find ways to use it all up at home. This recipe is great for this dilemma. Just cut it up into pieces, and let the blender do all the work for you.

serves: 10 ~ *hands-on:* 10 min. ~ *total:* 2 hr., 10 min.

1 (6-lb.) seedless watermelon

1 Tbsp. sugar

1½ cups chilled Lillet Blanc

¼ cup fresh lime juice (about 2 large limes)

1 (750-milliliter) bottle Prosecco, chilled

1. Remove rind from watermelon; cut flesh into large chunks. Process half of watermelon chunks in a blender 1 minute or until liquefied. Pour through a fine wire-mesh strainer into a large bowl, using the back of a spoon to squeeze out juice; discard pulp. Repeat procedure with remaining half of watermelon chunks.

2. Measure 3 cups watermelon juice, and pour into a 3-qt. pitcher. (Reserve remaining watermelon juice for another use.) Add sugar, stirring until dissolved. Cover and chill 2 hours.

3. Stir in Lillet Blanc and lime juice. Gently stir in Prosecco. Serve immediately.

KITCHEN TIP

Turn this into a kid-friendly watermelon punch by omitting the wine and substituting lemon-lime soda for the Prosecco.

Summer
SPARKLER

Growing up, the only fireworks that we got to handle, thank goodness, were the sparklers, and I still love them today. The little bubbles in Champagne and the way the light catches them remind me of those happy sparklers of my childhood.

serves: 8 ~ *hands-on:* 5 min. ~ *total:* 15 min.

¼ cup sugar

1 cup fresh raspberries

1 cup fresh blueberries

1 peach, thinly sliced

1 (750-milliliter) bottle Champagne or sparkling wine, chilled

1. Stir together sugar and ¼ cup water in a microwave-safe bowl. Microwave at HIGH 1 minute; stir until sugar dissolves. Cool 10 minutes.

2. Gently stir together sugar mixture, raspberries, blueberries, and peach slices in a large pitcher. Slowly pour in Champagne or sparkling wine.

Nothing says celebration quite like a glittering and glowing sparkler in one hand and a cup of berries and bubbly in the other.

Muscadine
SANGRÍA

Muscadines are regional grapes, native to the Southeast, that have thick skins and an unmistakable sweet, musky flavor. Using the wine made from them gives you all the flavor and a break from juicing the grapes. Muscadine wine is available in red or white, and you can find it in Southern wineries and some grocery stores, too. Its sweeter flavor profile makes it perfect for pairing with fresh fruit in a sangría.

serves: 10 ~ *hands-on:* 10 min. ~ *total:* 1 hr., 15 min.

½ cup brandy

¼ cup sugar

½ cantaloupe, seeded and cut lengthwise into 3 wedges

2 firm ripe peaches, unpeeled, pitted, and thinly sliced

1 lime, thinly sliced

1 Fuji apple, peeled and thinly sliced

3 Tbsp. fresh lime juice (about 2 limes)

1 (750-milliliter) bottle white muscadine wine, chilled

1 (750-milliliter) bottle Prosecco, chilled

1. Combine brandy and sugar in a large bowl or pitcher; let stand 5 minutes. Stir until sugar dissolves.

2. Meanwhile, peel cantaloupe wedges, and cut crosswise into thin slices to measure 3 cups; add to brandy mixture. Add peach, lime, and apple slices. Stir in lime juice and wine. Cover and chill at least 1 hour.

3. Gently stir in Prosecco. Serve immediately over ice.

NOTE: We tested with Tsali Notch Sweetwater Muscadine Wine.

―――――― ⌘ KITCHEN TIP ⌘ ――――――

Try the muscadine wine on its own
before making the sangría. If it's very sweet,
omit the added sugar in the recipe.

Grown-Up
SPARKLING CIDER

When I was little, even the children got to join in the festivities on New Year's Eve, but with a glass of sparkling cider instead of Champagne. I still like to toast with cider on the last day of the year, albeit with this grown-up version.

serves: 2 ~ *hands-on:* 5 min. ~ *total:* 5 min.

1 cup sparkling apple cider

6 Tbsp. bourbon

2 (½-inch-thick) Granny Smith apple wedges

1. Fill a large cocktail shaker half full of ice. Add apple cider and bourbon; cover and shake vigorously 30 seconds or until thoroughly chilled. Strain into 2 highball glasses. Add 1 apple wedge to each glass, and serve immediately.

⟅ KITCHEN TIP ⟆

To keep apple slices from turning
brown before adding to drinks, toss them in
a little fresh lemon juice.

Blackberry-Cucumber
SWEET TEA

Cucumbers have an incredible way of pairing with other vegetables and fruits, and they bring a cool and refreshing quality to anything that's made with them. For this fragrant drink, sweet blackberries complement the cucumber and create rich, vivid color. This is sweet tea like you've never tasted it before.

serves: 8 ~ *hands-on:* 9 min. ~ *total:* 2 hr., 19 min.

3 family-size black tea bags

1 medium cucumber (about 9 oz.)

2 cups fresh blackberries

½ cup sugar

5 cups ice water

1 Tbsp. fresh lemon juice (about 1 lemon)

Garnishes: fresh blackberries, cucumber slices, mint sprigs

1. Bring 3 cups water to a boil in a medium saucepan. Remove pan from heat; add tea bags, cover, and steep 10 minutes.

2. Meanwhile, peel cucumber; cut in half lengthwise, removing and discarding seeds. Chop cucumber halves. Process blackberries and cucumber in a blender until smooth, stopping to scrape down sides as needed. Pour mixture through a fine wire-mesh strainer into a large bowl; discard solids.

3. Remove tea bags from water; add sugar to hot tea, stirring to dissolve.

4. Pour tea mixture into large pitcher, and stir in ice water. Stir in blackberry mixture and lemon juice. Cover and chill 2 hours. Serve over ice.

Say farewell to typical iced tea. This simple drink makes friends and family feel like honored guests.

Raspberry-Orange
PUNCH

This drink is one of my son Kelly's favorites. Sometimes I make it with orange sherbet instead of raspberry sorbet, but it's always a win either way. Plus, it's so easy to whip together.

serves: 24 ~ *hands-on:* 10 min. ~ *total:* 10 min.

4 cups fresh orange juice (about 12 oranges)

2 pt. raspberry sorbet, softened

1 (2-liter) lemon-lime soft drink

Garnishes: fresh raspberries, orange slices

1. Combine first 3 ingredients in large punch bowl.

NOTE: We tested with Sprite.

KITCHEN TIP

Make colorful fruit kebabs as garnishes for these drinks.
Using small picks or swizzle sticks, thread orange
slices and berries in an alternating pattern.

Homemade Strawberry
MILK

Every spring, my son and I eagerly wait for Brown Farms in New Market, Alabama, to announce strawberry picking. We pick and buy many more strawberries than we could ever, ever, ever use! So, in a hurry before our strawberries perish, I make syrups, jams, and such. This is a great recipe for the kids, and it's always a huge hit. Try the strawberry syrup over ice cream, too!

serves: 2 ~ *hands-on:* 18 min. ~ *total:* 2 hr., 18 min.

1 cup fresh strawberries, chopped

½ cup sugar

1½ cups milk

Garnish: fresh strawberries

1. Freeze 2 small freezer-safe glasses 10 minutes.

2. Meanwhile, bring strawberries, sugar, and 1 cup water to a boil in a small saucepan; boil 10 minutes or until slightly thickened and reduced. Pour strawberry mixture through a fine wire-mesh strainer into a small bowl, reserving strawberries for another use. Cover syrup, and chill 2 hours.

3. Pour ¾ cup milk and 3 Tbsp. strawberry syrup into each frozen glass, stirring to blend. Refrigerate remaining syrup in an airtight container.

It's so easy to find ripe, juicy berries for Homemade Strawberry Milk. Fresh fruit takes a good-for-you drink and instantly makes it fun and special.

Buttermilk Scallion Cornbread

BEE HAPPY

Chapter

-5-

SUPPERTIME

The BLUE BO...
Tree...

Feast, Saturday!

I'm not sure the word "supper" is even used outside the South, but I think it's magical. Dinner can be formal and intimidating, but supper is a warm, culinary hug at the end of your day. Southerners hear "y'all come for supper," and they know they're being invited to a relaxed and welcoming meal where they will be treated like family. For me, evening time together at the table is sacred. At suppertime, my son and I sit down together and say three things we're thankful for. Kelly always says, "I'm thankful for you, me, and the beautiful day." We love to make our friends part of our family, and when we have them over for supper, we invite them to say "The Three Things" as well. Suppertime entrées and sides don't have to be overly complicated and difficult to prepare—they just have to be good! In this chapter, you'll find my favorite feast, as well as crowd-pleasing classics like Jambalaya and Hearty Beef & Beer Stew. Side dishes are low on the deep-fry but heavy on the Southern: Fig & Pork-Stuffed Acorn Squash, Summer Corn Risotto, and Buttermilk & Green Onion Cornbread, to name a few. My hope is to offer you lots of delicious choices that take the fuss out of evening meal plans. And I think we're all blessed when we take that special time at sundown to gather around the table and be thankful together—"for you, me, and the beautiful day."

SHRIMP BOIL

This is the kind of feast that you just have to roll up your sleeves and dig into. Invite your friends over, and serve this outside on a big table covered with newspaper or butcher paper.

serves: 8 ~ *hands-on:* 15 min. ~ *total:* 42 min.

1 lemon, quartered

5 Tbsp. Cajun seasoning

2 bay leaves

4 garlic cloves

1 lb. baby red potatoes

4 ears fresh corn, husks removed and broken in half

1 lb. andouille sausage, cut into 1-inch pieces

1½ lb. unpeeled large raw shrimp

⅓ cup mayonnaise

⅓ cup ketchup

1½ Tbsp. prepared horseradish

½ tsp. ground red pepper

1. Place 4 qt. water in a 6-qt. Dutch oven. Squeeze juice from lemon quarters into water, adding squeezed quarters to water. Add Cajun seasoning and next 3 ingredients.

2. Bring to a boil; partially cover, reduce heat, and simmer 10 minutes or until potatoes are slightly tender.

3. Increase heat to high. Add corn and sausage; bring to a simmer. Cook 4 minutes. Stir in shrimp, and cook 3 minutes or just until shrimp turn pink. Drain; remove and discard bay leaves and garlic.

4. Stir together mayonnaise and next 3 ingredients; serve with shrimp boil.

KITCHEN TIP

Along with the rémoulade sauce, place bowls of lemon wedges, bottles of hot sauce, and plenty of paper towels all around the table.

CATFISH FILLETS
with Mashed Lima Beans & Mint

My grandmother lived on Guntersville Lake, and I would spend my summer weekends jumping off her dock into the cool waters. I never tired of it! Twice each summer she hosted a fish fry with all of the fish caught off of the dock. Fried catfish will forever hold a special place in my heart, and pairing it with lima beans and fresh mint is an updated touch that's sure to please a crowd.

serves: 6 ~ *hands-on:* 22 min. ~ *total:* 22 min.

2½ cups frozen baby lima beans

3½ Tbsp. chopped fresh mint, divided

7 Tbsp. olive oil, divided

1 Tbsp. lemon zest, divided

1¾ tsp. kosher salt, divided

¼ tsp. freshly ground black pepper

6 (6-oz.) catfish fillets

¼ tsp. dried crushed red pepper

1 cup all-purpose flour

1. Cook lima beans in a large saucepan in boiling salted water to cover 4 minutes; drain, reserving 5 Tbsp. cooking liquid. Process lima beans, reserved cooking liquid, 2 Tbsp. mint, 3 Tbsp. oil, 1 tsp. lemon zest, ¼ tsp. salt, and black pepper. Keep warm.

2. Place fish on a large rimmed baking sheet. Combine ¼ tsp. dried crushed red pepper, remaining 1½ Tbsp. mint, remaining 2 tsp. lemon zest, and remaining 1½ tsp. salt in small bowl. Rub mint mixture over fish.

3. Place flour in a large shallow dish. Dredge fish in flour, shaking off excess. Heat 2 Tbsp. oil in a large nonstick skillet over medium-high heat. Fry half of fish in hot oil 3 minutes on each side or until lightly browned. Drain on paper towels. Repeat procedure with remaining 2 Tbsp. oil and remaining half of fish.

4. Place ⅓ cup lima bean mixture on each of 6 plates. Top each with 1 fish fillet. Serve immediately.

KITCHEN TIP

You can make these mashed lima beans ahead. Just reheat them in the microwave, and wait to stir in the mint just before serving.

Spicy Ginger-Chicken
LETTUCE WRAPS

These wraps are the epitome of a fast and fresh meal, perfect to serve buffet style so family and friends can assemble their own. Nothing is more fun for me than watching hands reaching for all the tempting options as conversation is flying.

serves: 6 ~ *hands-on:* 12 min. ~ *total:* 25 min.

2½ Tbsp. sugar

2½ Tbsp. fish sauce

2½ Tbsp. fresh lime juice (about 3 limes)

1 tsp. dried crushed red pepper

2 Tbsp. vegetable oil

2 lb. ground chicken

¼ cup minced fresh ginger

8 large green onions, finely chopped

4 garlic cloves, minced

2 small jalapeño peppers, seeded and finely chopped

¼ cup chopped fresh cilantro

2 large heads Boston or Bibb lettuce, separated into leaves

1. Combine first 4 ingredients in a microwave-safe bowl. Microwave at HIGH 20 seconds; stir until sugar dissolves.

2. Heat oil in a large skillet over high heat. Brown chicken in hot oil, stirring often, 7 minutes or until chicken crumbles and is desired degree of doneness. Add ginger and next 3 ingredients; sauté 2 minutes. Stir in ¼ cup fish sauce mixture. Remove skillet from heat. Stir in cilantro. Spoon chicken mixture into lettuce leaves. Serve with remaining ¼ cup fish sauce mixture.

MARKET TIP

You can find fish sauce in the international aisle of most supermarkets. It adds a depth of flavor to recipes like stir-fries and sauces.

Classic Chicken
POT PIES

If you want to make a comforting pot pie but don't have much time, look no further than these mini pot pies. Thanks to precooked chicken, you can have these on the table in less than an hour.

serves: 4 ~ *hands-on:* 23 min. ~ *total:* 58 min.

½ recipe Basic Pie Crust (page 281)

6 Tbsp. butter

1 cup chopped onion

1 cup diced carrot

½ cup chopped celery

½ tsp. table salt

½ tsp. freshly ground black pepper

½ tsp. dried thyme

6 Tbsp. all-purpose flour

2 cups chicken stock

1 cup milk

2 cups shredded cooked chicken

1 cup frozen English peas

2 Tbsp. finely chopped fresh parsley

1. Prepare Basic Pie Crust through Step 3.

2. Preheat oven to 400°. Place 4 (2-cup) ramekins on a baking sheet.

3. Melt butter in a Dutch oven over medium-high heat. Add onion, carrot, and celery; sauté 5 minutes. Stir in salt, pepper, and thyme. Stir in flour; cook, stirring constantly, 3 minutes. Gradually stir in chicken stock. Bring to a boil; reduce heat, and simmer 2 minutes or until mixture begins to thicken. Stir in milk; cook, stirring occasionally, 4 minutes. Stir in chicken, peas, and parsley. Pour into ramekins.

4. Roll dough to ⅛-inch thickness. Cut dough into 4 rounds using a 5-inch round cutter and rerolling dough twice. Place dough rounds over filling; crimp edges of dough to edges of ramekins to seal. Cut slits in top for steam to escape.

5. Bake at 400° for 30 minutes or until crust is golden brown and crisp. Cool on a wire rack 5 minutes before serving.

KITCHEN TIP

For the cooked chicken, I recommend buying a rotisserie chicken from the deli section of your grocery. Shred it into bite-size pieces using two forks.

Mushroom & Chicken
MEATBALLS

The secret to good chicken meatballs is making sure they are packed with flavor. I think mushrooms and a touch of Parmesan do the trick. Serve these over spaghetti with your favorite pasta sauce, or add them to your own homemade vegetable soup.

serves: 4 ~ *hands-on:* 18 min. ~ *total:* 18 min.

8 large fresh mushrooms

3 large green onions, cut crosswise into thirds

1 large garlic clove

½ tsp. kosher salt

¼ tsp. freshly ground black pepper

1 lb. ground chicken

2 Tbsp. freshly grated Parmesan cheese

1 large egg, beaten

3 Tbsp. olive oil

1. Pulse first 5 ingredients in a food processor until vegetables are finely chopped.

2. Place chicken and next 2 ingredients in a bowl. Stir in mushroom mixture just until blended. Shape into 24 balls.

3. Heat oil in a large nonstick skillet over medium heat 1 minute. Add meatballs, and cook, turning to brown on all sides, 4 minutes or until desired degree of doneness.

Peanutty BRAISED CHICKEN

Peanut butter gives this dish exotic flavor and creates a velvety sauce when combined with tomatoes. I like to serve it over basmati rice and pile on the toppings: green onions, cilantro, and lots of crunchy peanuts.

serves: 6 ~ *hands-on:* 34 min. ~ *total:* 34 min.

1 cup creamy peanut butter

1½ cups chicken broth, warmed

2 lb. skinned and boned chicken breasts, cut into ½-inch cubes

1¼ tsp. kosher salt, divided

2 Tbsp. vegetable oil

1 medium onion, chopped

1 red bell pepper, chopped

3 garlic cloves, finely chopped

1 (14.5-oz.) can diced tomatoes, undrained

Hot cooked rice

Toppings: sliced green onions, fresh cilantro leaves, chopped peanuts

1. Place peanut butter in a medium bowl; gradually whisk in chicken broth until blended.

2. Pat chicken dry with paper towels; sprinkle with 1 tsp. salt, and toss well. Heat oil in a 4- to 5-qt. heavy ovenproof Dutch oven over medium-high heat. Brown chicken, in batches, in hot oil 3-5 minutes. Transfer to a bowl.

3. Add onion and bell pepper to Dutch oven; sauté 4 minutes or until onion begins to brown. Add garlic; sauté 1 minute. Stir in chicken along with any accumulated juices, peanut butter mixture, tomatoes, and remaining ¼ tsp. salt. Bring to a simmer; reduce heat to low, and simmer 10 minutes or until desired degree of doneness.

4. Serve chicken mixture over rice. Sprinkle with toppings.

Easy Chicken POSOLE

Whether you call it "posole" or "pozole," it always sounds delicious to me. Hominy is the signature ingredient here; it's made from corn and has a mildness that's perfect for picking up the rich and smoky flavors of the soup. Serve this any time of the year with a loaf of hearty bread.

serves: 6-8 ~ *hands-on:* 44 min. ~ *total:* 49 min.

1 Tbsp. olive oil

2 medium onions, chopped

⅓ cup tomato paste

3 Tbsp. chili powder

8 garlic cloves, minced

4 (15-oz.) cans white hominy, drained

1 (32-oz.) container chicken broth

2½ cups shredded deli-roasted chicken

½ tsp. kosher salt

½ tsp. freshly ground black pepper

1½ cups shredded lettuce

1½ cups (6 oz.) shredded Monterey Jack cheese

¾ cup sliced radishes

¾ cup sliced green onions

1. Heat oil in a 5-qt. Dutch oven over medium heat. Add onion; sauté 3 minutes. Add tomato paste, chili powder, and garlic. Cook, stirring constantly, until blended.

2. Add hominy, broth, and 2 cups water. Bring to a boil; reduce heat, and simmer, uncovered, 30 minutes, stirring occasionally.

3. Stir in chicken, salt, and pepper. Cook 5 minutes or until thoroughly heated. Ladle soup into bowls; top evenly with lettuce and remaining ingredients.

Cajun DIRTY RICE

The foundation of flavor for this recipe, as in most Cajun dishes, is the "trinity" of celery, onions, and peppers. Along with ground pork and chicken livers, the trinity gets browned in the skillet, providing even more flavor. I like to top it off with torn celery leaves to give a hint of freshness to this classic dish.

serves: 6-8 ~ *hands-on:* 32 min. ~ *total:* 35 min.

1 Tbsp. vegetable oil

4 oz. chicken livers

4 oz. ground pork

1 tsp. kosher salt

½ tsp. freshly ground black pepper

½ tsp. chili powder

1½ cups chicken broth, divided

1 small onion, chopped

2 celery ribs, chopped

3 garlic cloves, minced

1 small jalapeño pepper, seeded and chopped

2 tsp. dried oregano

3 cups cooked long-grain rice

⅔ cup chopped green onions

2 Tbsp. chopped fresh parsley

Garnish: celery leaves

1. Heat oil in a large skillet over medium-high heat. Add chicken livers; cook 3 minutes or until browned. Remove chicken livers from skillet. Let stand until cool enough to handle; chop.

2. Add pork to skillet; cook, stirring to crumble, 4 minutes or just until beginning to brown. Stir in chopped chicken livers, salt, pepper, and chili powder; cook, stirring occasionally, 2 minutes.

3. Add ¼ cup chicken broth, and cook 3 minutes or until broth evaporates and meat mixture is browned, crusty, and slightly sticks to skillet. Add onion and next 4 ingredients. Cook, stirring occasionally, 7 minutes or until vegetables are browned, crusty, and slightly stick to skillet.

4. Add rice, green onions, parsley, and remaining 1¼ cups broth. Cook, stirring occasionally, 5 minutes or until liquid is absorbed and rice is thoroughly heated.

Deconstructed Chicken
POT PIE

I love to make all kinds of pot pies: mini pies, savory hand pies, and this luscious interpretation that takes apart all the elements and stacks them up into a beautiful presentation.

serves: 9 ~ hands-on: 56 min. ~ total: 1 hr., 31 min.

½ (17.3-oz.) package frozen puff pastry sheets, thawed

7 Tbsp. butter, divided

1 onion, chopped

1 lb. celery root, cut into 1-inch pieces

1 garlic clove, crushed

½ cup dry white wine

1 medium potato, peeled and cut into 1-inch pieces

3 cups chicken broth, divided

1 tsp. table salt, divided

1 tsp. freshly ground black pepper, divided

1 Tbsp. chopped fresh parsley

4 large carrots, peeled and diced

1 Tbsp. chopped fresh thyme

¼ cup all-purpose flour

½ cup milk

4 oz. blue cheese, crumbled

4 cups chopped cooked chicken

Garnish: fresh thyme leaves

1. Preheat oven to 400°. On a lightly floured surface, cut pastry sheet into 9 squares. Place squares on an ungreased baking sheet. Bake for 15 minutes or until golden brown.

2. Melt 2 Tbsp. butter in a large saucepan over medium-high heat. Add onion, celery root, and garlic; sauté over medium-high heat 8 minutes or until onion is tender. Stir in wine; cook 2 minutes or until reduced by half. Add potato and 1 cup chicken broth. Bring to a boil over medium-high heat; reduce heat, and simmer, uncovered, 20 minutes or until vegetables are tender. Place vegetables in a food processor; process until smooth. Stir in ¼ tsp. salt, ¼ tsp. pepper, and parsley. Keep warm.

3. Melt 1 Tbsp. butter in a large skillet over medium-high heat. Add carrot, thyme, ¼ tsp. salt, and ¼ tsp. pepper. Cook, stirring occasionally, 7 minutes or until lightly browned. Transfer to a bowl; set aside.

4. Melt remaining ¼ cup butter in a heavy saucepan over low heat; whisk in flour until smooth. Cook 1 minute, whisking constantly. Gradually whisk in milk and remaining 2 cups chicken broth; cook over medium-high heat, whisking constantly, until mixture is thickened and bubbly. Add blue cheese, remaining ½ tsp. salt, and remaining ½ tsp. pepper, stirring until cheese melts. Stir in carrot mixture and chicken; cook until heated through.

5. Split pastry squares. Spoon about ⅓ cup celery root puree onto each of 9 plates. Top each with 1 pastry bottom and about ½ cup chicken filling. Cover each with 1 pastry top. Serve immediately.

Chili Verde
BRAISED PORK

Although chili verde is probably most familiar as a hearty stew, I like to use the same ingredients and cooking technique to prepare pork shoulder. The secret to the tenderness is to let the meat simmer in cola made with cane syrup. The bright tomatillos and smoky poblanos give this dish its signature green hue and balance out the richness of the pork.

makes: 11 cups ~ *hands-on:* 40 min. ~ *total:* 1 hr., 40 min.

1 (3-lb.) boneless pork shoulder roast
   (Boston butt)

¼ cup olive oil

2 large yellow onions, chopped

3 poblano peppers, seeded and chopped

2 jalapeño peppers, seeded and minced

4 garlic cloves

1 (8-oz.) bottle cola soft drink

2 cups chicken stock

1 Tbsp. kosher salt

1 Tbsp. dried oregano

1 Tbsp. ground cumin

1 Tbsp. freshly ground black pepper

1 (16-oz.) jar tomatillo salsa

1 cup coarsely chopped fresh cilantro

Flour tortillas, warmed

Pico de gallo

1. Trim fat from pork; cut pork into 1-inch cubes. Heat 2 Tbsp. oil in a large Dutch oven over medium heat. Add half of pork; cook 5 minutes or until browned on all sides. Remove pork from Dutch oven, and place on a plate. Repeat procedure with remaining oil and pork.

2. Sauté onion and next 3 ingredients in hot drippings 4 minutes or until translucent. Return pork and any accumulated juices to Dutch oven. Add cola, and cook 5 minutes, stirring to loosen browned bits from bottom of Dutch oven.

3. Stir in stock and next 5 ingredients. Bring to a boil; reduce heat, partially cover, and simmer, stirring occasionally, 1 hour or until pork is fork tender.

4. Remove from heat, and stir in cilantro. Serve with warm tortillas and pico de gallo.

NOTE: *We tested with Frontera Gourmet Mexican Tomatillo Salsa.*

Fig & Pork-Stuffed
ACORN SQUASH

Using the squash halves as individual serving dishes keeps the stuffing moist and flavorful while making a beautifully rustic presentation. I serve these as a light dinner along with a salad or as an appetizer for a holiday feast.

serves: 8 ~ hands-on: 30 min. ~ total: 1 hr., 30 min.

4 large acorn squash (about 7½ lb.), halved lengthwise

12 oz. ground pork sausage

1 cup chopped onion

4 cups (½-inch) rustic bread cubes, toasted

1½ cups chicken broth

¾ cup chopped dried figs

½ cup coarsely chopped pecans, toasted

2 tsp. fresh thyme leaves

½ tsp. table salt

½ tsp. freshly ground black pepper

1 large egg, lightly beaten

Garnishes: fresh parsley leaves, fresh thyme leaves

1. Preheat oven to 400°. Scoop out pulp and seeds from squash halves with a spoon; reserve seeds for another use, and discard pulp. Cut a thin slice from skin sides of squash halves so they will sit flat, being careful not to cut into flesh. Place halves, cut sides up, in 2 (13- x 9-inch) baking dishes.

2. Brown sausage in a large nonstick skillet over medium-high heat, stirring often, 8 minutes or until sausage crumbles. Drain sausage, and place in a large bowl, reserving drippings in skillet. Sauté onion in hot drippings 3-5 minutes or until tender. Add onion to sausage. Stir in bread and next 7 ingredients.

3. Spoon stuffing into squash halves. Cover loosely with aluminum foil. Bake at 400° for 1 hour or until squash is tender. Serve immediately.

MARKET TIP

When buying acorn squash, choose those that are solid and heavy. The skin of the squash should be deeply colored with a matte finish.

Stuffed Poblano PEPPERS

Stuffed peppers are pretty popular on both the Greek and the Southern sides of my family. Many people are used to the stuffed bell pepper, but I much prefer using poblanos instead. I serve these as a main dish paired with Grilled Spring Onion Trio (page 245).

serves: 6 ~ *hands-on:* 19 min. ~ *total:* 1 hr., 9 min.

2 (8-oz.) cans tomato sauce with roasted garlic

2 canned chipotle peppers in adobo sauce

¾ tsp. kosher salt, divided

¾ tsp. freshly ground black pepper, divided

¾ cup drained black beans

¾ cup frozen roasted whole kernel corn, thawed

¾ cup cooked long-grain rice

¾ cup shredded smoked pork

½ cup finely chopped onion

2 Tbsp. chopped fresh cilantro

1 Tbsp. fresh lime juice (about 1 large lime)

½ tsp. ground cumin

1 garlic clove, minced

¾ cup shredded quesadilla cheese, divided

3 large poblano peppers

1 cup Mexican crema

Garnish: fresh cilantro sprigs

1. Preheat oven to 425°. Preheat grill to 450°-500° (high) heat. Process tomato sauce, chipotle chiles, ½ tsp. salt, and ½ tsp. pepper in a food processor until smooth. Spread 1½ cups sauce mixture in bottom of a 13- x 9-inch baking dish.

2. Combine beans, next 8 ingredients, ½ cup cheese, remaining ¼ tsp. salt, remaining ¼ tsp. pepper, and remaining ½ cup sauce mixture in a medium bowl.

3. Grill peppers, covered with grill lid, 3-4 minutes on each side or until lightly charred. Cut peppers in half; discard seeds and membranes. Stuff pepper halves evenly with pork mixture; place on top of sauce mixture in baking dish.

4. Cover and bake at 425° for 45 minutes. Uncover, sprinkle with remaining ¼ cup cheese, and bake 5 more minutes or until cheese is brown. Drizzle with crema.

JAMBALAYA
with Shrimp & Andouille Sausage

I've always been a big fan of jambalaya, with its bold Creole flavors and its ability to accommodate almost any kind of meat. I think what stops most people from making it at home is the fear that the rice won't get cooked properly. Here is the key: Once the rice gets cooking, keep the pot covered until the 15 minutes is up; then check to make sure the rice is tender before adding in the remaining ingredients.

serves: 4 ~ *hands-on:* 26 min. ~ *total:* 41 min.

½ lb. large raw shrimp, peeled, deveined, and chopped

4 oz. skinned and boned chicken breasts, diced

1 Tbsp. Creole seasoning, divided

8 oz. andouille sausage

2 Tbsp. olive oil, divided

1 cup chopped onion

¾ cup chopped green bell pepper

⅔ cup chopped celery

1 cup chopped tomato

1 tsp. Worcestershire sauce

1 tsp. hot sauce

3 large garlic cloves, minced

3 bay leaves

1 cup uncooked long-grain rice

2½ cups chicken broth

Garnish: fresh flat-leaf parsley sprigs

1. Combine shrimp, chicken, and 1½ tsp. Creole seasoning, tossing to coat. Cut sausage in half lengthwise; cut crosswise into ½-inch slices.

2. Heat 1 Tbsp. oil in a Dutch oven over medium-high heat. Add sausage, and cook 3 minutes or until browned, stirring occasionally.

3. Add shrimp mixture; cook 3 minutes or until shrimp turns pink and chicken is desired degree of doneness. Transfer to a plate using a slotted spoon.

4. Heat remaining 1 Tbsp. oil in Dutch oven. Add onion, bell pepper, and celery; sauté 5 minutes or until tender. Add tomato, next 4 ingredients, and remaining 1½ tsp. Creole seasoning.

5. Stir in rice. Gradually stir in broth. Bring to a boil; cover, reduce heat to medium-low, and cook 15 minutes or until liquid is absorbed and rice is tender.

6. Add shrimp mixture; cook 1 minute or until thoroughly heated. Remove and discard bay leaves.

Hearty Beef & Beer
STEW

This is an old-fashioned beef stew inspired by a version my grandmother used to make, but updated with stout beer and sweet potatoes. Just a dash of allspice gives this dish a hint of warm spice that will make your guests say MMMMMM.

makes: 13 cups ~ *hands-on:* 20 min. ~ *total:* 2 hr., 20 min.

⅓ cup all-purpose flour

1½ tsp. kosher salt, divided

½ tsp. freshly ground black pepper, divided

2 lb. beef stew meat

¼ cup shortening

1 (12-oz.) bottle stout beer

1 Tbsp. fresh lemon juice (about 1 lemon)

1 Tbsp. Worcestershire sauce

1 tsp. sugar

¼ tsp. ground allspice

2 bay leaves

1 large onion, vertically sliced

1½ lb. sweet potatoes (about 2 potatoes), peeled and cut into 1-inch chunks

12 small pearl onions, peeled

6 small carrots, cut into 2-inch pieces

Garnish: chopped fresh parsley

1. Combine flour, 1 tsp. salt, and ¼ tsp. pepper in a large heavy-duty zip-top plastic freezer bag. Add half of beef; seal bag, and shake to coat. Melt shortening in a Dutch oven over medium-high heat. Remove beef from bag, shaking off excess flour; add to hot shortening. Cook, stirring occasionally, 8 minutes or until browned. Transfer beef to a large plate. Repeat procedure with remaining half of beef. Return beef to Dutch oven.

2. Add beer to drippings, stirring to loosen browned bits from bottom of Dutch oven. Add 3 cups water. Stir in lemon juice, next 5 ingredients, remaining ½ tsp. salt, and remaining ¼ tsp. pepper. Bring to a boil; cover, reduce heat, and simmer 1½ hours or until beef is tender.

3. Add sweet potato, pearl onions, and carrot. Return to a boil; cover, reduce heat, and simmer 30 minutes or until vegetables are tender. Remove and discard bay leaves.

NOTE: We tested with Guinness Draught Stout Beer.

Root Vegetable & Sirloin
POT PIE

Surely by now, you can tell I have an affinity for pot pies! This one made with sirloin is packed with root vegetables such as parsnips and rutabagas, as well as carrots and onions. It's a hearty meal perfect for entertaining during chilly winter months.

serves: 8 ~ *hands-on:* 1 hr., 29 min. ~ *total:* 2 hr., 29 min.

1 Tbsp. olive oil

1 (3-lb.) top sirloin roast, trimmed and cut into 1-inch pieces

2 cups cubed peeled rutabaga

½ lb. parsnips, peeled and cut into ½-inch pieces

2 onions, chopped

4 carrots, cut into ½-inch pieces

3 garlic cloves, minced

½ cup bourbon

3 cups beef stock

2 Tbsp. chopped fresh thyme

2½ tsp. kosher salt

1 tsp. freshly ground black pepper

1 bay leaf

3 Tbsp. all-purpose flour

1 (17.3-oz.) package frozen puff pastry sheets, thawed

1. Heat 1 Tbsp. oil in a Dutch oven over medium-high heat. Add beef; cook in batches, turning to brown on all sides, about 4 minutes; transfer beef to a large plate once browned.

2. Add rutabaga and next 3 ingredients to Dutch oven. Cook, stirring occasionally, 8 minutes or until browned. Stir in garlic, and cook 1 minute. Return beef to pan. Add bourbon, and cook 2 minutes, stirring to loosen browned bits from bottom of Dutch oven. Add beef stock and next 4 ingredients. Bring to a simmer over medium-low heat, and simmer 40 minutes or until vegetables and meat are tender, stirring occasionally.

3. Preheat oven to 400°. Whisk together flour and ¼ cup water in a small bowl; gradually stir flour mixture into beef mixture. Bring to a boil over medium-high heat; cook 2-3 minutes or until thickened. Spoon beef mixture evenly into 8 (12-oz.) ovenproof bowls. Set bowls on a large rimmed baking sheet.

4. Unfold each pastry sheet on a lightly floured surface. Roll sheets into 10-inch squares. Cut each square into 4 (5-inch) squares. Cut slits or decorative shapes in squares with small hors d'oeuvre cutters. Place puff pastry squares on top of bowls. Gently press pastry edges over edges of bowls.

5. Bake at 400° for 20 minutes or until crusts are golden brown and filling is bubbly.

A HEARTY
Feast

SERVES 6

The Presbyterian

Cowboy Steaks with Jalapeño Butter

Creamed Kale

Roasted Beets

Potato & Leek Gratin

Arborio Rice Pudding Brûlée

You don't have to wait until the holidays to gather friends and family for a sit-down dinner. The trick to this menu? Buy large steaks you can slice to serve a crowd, and pair with hearty sides and a decadent dessert.

The Presbyterian

Roasted Beets

Potato & Leek Gratin

❧ ENTERTAINING TIP ❧

Set a welcoming dinner table:

- Choose small flower arrangements and low centerpieces that don't block conversation
- Balance neutral tableware with a few pops of color
- Place carafes or bottles of water around the table for easy replenishment
- Provide flatware appropriate for your menu, such as steak knives or fish forks

Cowboy Steaks with Jalapeño Butter

Arborio Rice Pudding Brûlée

The Presbyterian

serves: 1 ~ *hands-on:* 15 min.
total: 1 hr., 30 min.

CANDIED GINGER AND GINGER SYRUP

½ lb. fresh ginger, peeled and very thinly
   sliced (about 1⅓ cups)

1½ cups sugar, divided

⅛ tsp. table salt

THE PRESBYTERIAN

¼ cup bourbon

1 Tbsp. Candied Ginger

1½ tsp. Ginger Syrup

2 dashes of Angostura bitters

¼ cup club soda

Garnish: Candied Ginger

1. Prepare Candied Ginger and Ginger Syrup:
Bring ginger slices and 1 cup water to a boil
in a medium saucepan; reduce heat, and simmer, uncovered, 15 minutes. Drain.

2. Combine 1 cup sugar, salt, and 1 cup water
in same pan. Cook over medium-high heat until sugar dissolves, stirring once. Reduce heat
to medium; add ginger slices, and cook 30
minutes or until syrup resembles thin honey.

3. Remove pan from heat, and pour mixture
through a fine wire-mesh strainer into a
bowl, reserving ginger slices and syrup. Place
remaining ½ cup sugar in a shallow dish; add
ginger slices, tossing to coat. Let ginger stand

in sugar 30 minutes. Shake off excess sugar,
and transfer candied ginger to an airtight
container. Store at room temperature up to 3
months. Transfer Ginger Syrup to an airtight
container, and refrigerate up to 2 weeks.

4. Prepare The Presbyterian: Muddle bourbon
and next 3 ingredients in a highball glass to
release flavors. Fill glass with ice; gently stir
in club soda.

Cowboy Steaks with Jalapeño Butter

serves: 6 ~ *hands-on:* 20 min.
total: 30 min.

¼ cup butter, softened

½ jalapeño pepper, seeded and finely chopped

1 garlic clove, minced

3 (1¼-lb.) bone-in rib-eye steaks

¾ tsp. kosher salt

1½ tsp. freshly ground black pepper

1. Preheat grill to 350°–400° (medium-high)
heat. Stir together first 3 ingredients in a bowl.

2. Sprinkle each steak with ¼ tsp. salt and
½ tsp. pepper. Grill, covered with grill lid,
3-4 minutes on each side or to desired
degree of doneness. Remove from grill;
let stand 10 minutes. Cut steaks diagonally
into thin slices. Divide steak slices evenly
among 6 plates. Top each serving with 1
Tbsp. butter mixture.

Creamed Kale

serves: 6 ~ *hands-on:* 51 min.
total: 56 min.

2 large bunches kale (about 1½ lb.)

5 thick hickory-smoked bacon slices,
   cut crosswise into ½-inch pieces

2 large shallots, finely chopped

3 Tbsp. all-purpose flour

2 cups milk

2 cups heavy cream

½ cup (2 oz.) freshly grated Parmesan cheese

½ tsp. kosher salt

1 tsp. freshly ground black pepper

1. Remove center stems from kale. Cut leaves crosswise into ½-inch strips. Cook kale in boiling salted water to cover 4 minutes or until beginning to wilt; drain. Plunge kale into ice water to stop the cooking process. Let stand 5 minutes; drain and pat dry with paper towels.

2. Cook bacon in a Dutch oven over medium heat 5 minutes or until crisp. Remove bacon from Dutch oven using a slotted spoon; reserve drippings in Dutch oven.

3. Cook shallots in hot drippings, stirring occasionally, 3 minutes or until tender. Add flour; cook, stirring constantly, 1 minute. Whisk in milk and cream; bring to a boil, whisking often. Add cheese, stirring until melted.

4. Stir in kale; reduce heat to low. Simmer 20 minutes or until kale is tender and sauce thickens. Stir in salt and pepper. Serve sprinkled with reserved bacon.

Roasted Beets

serves: 6 ~ *hands-on:* 15 min.
total: 1 hr., 45 min.

15 baby beets (about 1¼ lb.)

6 Tbsp. extra virgin olive oil, divided

2 large Vidalia onions or sweet onions, cut
   into ½-inch wedges

½ tsp. kosher salt, divided

½ tsp. freshly ground black pepper, divided

1 Tbsp. balsamic vinegar

1 tsp. minced fresh oregano

1 tsp. fresh thyme leaves

4 oz. goat cheese, crumbled

1. Preheat oven to 400°. Place beets on a baking sheet; drizzle with 2 Tbsp. oil, tossing to coat. Place onion wedges in a single layer on a separate baking sheet. Drizzle wedges with 2 Tbsp. oil, and sprinkle with ¼ tsp. salt and ¼ tsp. pepper.

2. Bake beets at 400° for 1 hour or until tender, adding pan with onion to oven during last 30 minutes of cooking.

3. Remove vegetables from oven, and let stand until beets are cool enough to handle (about 30 minutes). Peel beets, and cut in half. Place beets in a large bowl.

4. Whisk together vinegar, oregano, thyme, remaining 2 Tbsp. oil, remaining ¼ tsp. salt, and remaining ¼ tsp. pepper in a small bowl. Add vinaigrette to beets, tossing to coat.

5. Arrange beets on a serving platter; top with onion. Sprinkle with cheese.

Potato & Leek Gratin

serves: 8-10 ~ *hands-on:* 10 min.
total: 1 hr.

Vegetable cooking spray

3 small leeks

1 lb. Yukon gold potatoes, thinly sliced

12 oz. sweet potatoes, peeled and thinly sliced

1 Tbsp. chopped fresh thyme

1 Tbsp. extra virgin olive oil

1 tsp. kosher salt

½ tsp. freshly ground black pepper

1½ cups heavy whipping cream

6 oz. Gruyère cheese, shredded

1. Preheat oven to 350°. Lightly grease a 13- x 9-inch baking dish with cooking spray.

2. Remove and discard root ends and dark green tops of leeks. Cut in half lengthwise, and rinse thoroughly under cold running water to remove grit and sand.

3. Toss together leeks, potatoes, and next 5 ingredients in a large bowl. Spread vegetable mixture in an even layer in prepared baking dish. Pour cream over vegetable mixture.

4. Cover and bake at 350° for 30 minutes. Increase oven temperature to 400°. Uncover, and sprinkle with cheese.

5. Bake, uncovered, at 400° for 20 minutes or until bubbly and golden brown.

Arborio Rice Pudding Brûlée

serves: 6 ~ *hands-on:* 1 hr., 5 min.
total: 5 hr., 5 min.

5½ cups milk

¾ cup Arborio rice (short grain), rinsed

¾ cup pure maple syrup

⅛ tsp. table salt

½ tsp. vanilla extract

⅛ tsp. ground cinnamon

6 Tbsp. sugar

1. Combine first 4 ingredients in a medium saucepan. Bring to a boil over medium-high heat, stirring often; reduce heat, and simmer, uncovered, 38 minutes or until thickened, most of liquid is absorbed, and rice is tender, stirring occasionally. Stir in vanilla and cinnamon.

2. Divide rice pudding evenly among 6 (8-oz.) ramekins or (¾-cup) brûlée dishes. Place heavy-duty plastic wrap directly on warm pudding (to prevent a film from forming); chill 4 hours or overnight. (Pudding will thicken as it cools.)

3. Remove plastic wrap, and sprinkle top of each serving with 1 Tbsp. sugar. Caramelize sugar using a kitchen torch, holding torch 1-2 inches from top of pudding, and moving torch back and forth. Serve immediately.

Grilled Spring
ONION TRIO

This recipe couldn't be lovelier in its simplicity. Serve it with roasted meats as a beautiful and light side dish.

serves: 4 ~ *hands-on:* 9 min. ~ *total:* 15 min.

2 small leeks

2 bunches green onions (about 18 onions)

2 bunches (1½ lb.) baby Vidalia onions with tops, halved lengthwise

2½ Tbsp. olive oil, divided

½ tsp. kosher salt, divided

½ tsp. freshly ground black pepper, divided

1 Tbsp. fresh lemon juice (about 1 small lemon)

1 oz. crumbled goat cheese

1. Preheat grill to 450°-500° (high) heat.

2. Remove and discard root ends and dark green tops of leeks. Cut in half lengthwise, and rinse thoroughly under cold running water to remove grit and sand.

3. Drizzle leeks, green onions, and baby onions with 1 Tbsp. oil; sprinkle with ¼ tsp. salt and ¼ tsp. pepper.

4. Place onions on grill rack. Grill green onions and Vidalia onions, covered with grill lid, 3 minutes, turning once. Grill leeks, covered with grill lid, 6 minutes, turning once.

5. Whisk together lemon juice, remaining 1½ Tbsp. oil, remaining ¼ tsp. salt, and remaining ¼ tsp. pepper. Drizzle over grilled onions. Sprinkle with cheese.

Roasted
BRUSSELS SPROUTS

This recipe works with nearly any "wintry" vegetable like parsnips, carrots, or even beets, but I love the way Brussels sprouts get crispy when they are roasted like this. The pecans add a bit of crunch, too. This makes for a quick and easy side dish for busy weeknights.

serves: 5 ~ *hands-on:* 14 min. ~ *total:* 34 min.

2 lb. Brussels sprouts

6 Tbsp. olive oil

½ tsp. kosher salt

½ tsp. freshly ground black pepper

5 Tbsp. butter

1 cup chopped pecans

1 tsp. lemon zest

1 Tbsp. fresh lemon juice (about 1 lemon)

1. Preheat oven to 450°. Remove discolored leaves from Brussels sprouts. Cut off stem ends; cut sprouts in half, and place in a large bowl. Add oil, salt, and pepper, tossing to coat; place in a single layer on a rimmed baking sheet.

2. Bake at 450° for 20 minutes or just until tender and browned, stirring halfway through. Remove from oven; transfer Brussels sprouts to a bowl.

3. Melt butter in a medium nonstick skillet over medium heat. Sauté pecans in butter 3-5 minutes or until butter is brown and pecans are toasted. Remove from heat. Stir in lemon zest and lemon juice; add to Brussels sprouts, tossing to coat.

GREEN BEANS
with Gribiche Sauce

Gribiche sauce is a mixture of mayonnaise, lots of fresh herbs, chopped eggs, capers, pickles, and more. It makes everything from steamed vegetables to sautéed fish taste delectable, especially these green beans.

serves: 8 ~ *hands-on:* 10 min. ~ *total:* 22 min.

1 lb. fresh thin green beans, trimmed

2 Tbsp. capers, drained

1 Tbsp. chopped fresh chives

1 Tbsp. chopped fresh parsley

1 Tbsp. chopped fresh chervil

1 Tbsp. chopped fresh tarragon

½ tsp. table salt

¼ tsp. freshly ground black pepper

6 small sweet gherkin pickles, diced

2 large hard-cooked eggs, peeled and chopped

1¼ cups mayonnaise

¼ cup red wine vinegar

1. Cook green beans in boiling salted water to cover in a Dutch oven 4 minutes or until crisp-tender; drain. Plunge beans into ice water to stop the cooking process; drain.

2. Place capers and next 8 ingredients in a medium bowl. Add mayonnaise and vinegar, stirring until blended. Place green beans on a serving platter. Drizzle sauce over green beans, and serve immediately.

 MARKET TIP

The thin green beans in this recipe are much more tender and delicately flavored than string green beans; plus, you don't have to remove any strings. Sometimes they are labeled as "haricots verts."

Summer SUCCOTASH

Succotash is a wonderful way to try all the summery vegetables from the farmer's market in one dish. If you have a little bacon grease on hand, substitute it for the olive oil, and you won't be disappointed.

serves: 8 ~ *hands-on:* 16 min. ~ *total:* 31 min.

2 Tbsp. extra virgin olive oil

1½ cups chopped onion

1 large garlic clove, minced

2½ cups chopped tomatoes (about 1½ lb.)

2 cups fresh corn kernels (about 3 ears)

2 cups fresh or frozen baby lima beans, thawed

1 tsp. kosher salt

½ tsp. freshly ground black pepper

3 Tbsp. torn fresh basil

1. Heat oil in a large heavy skillet over medium heat. Add onion, and sauté 5 minutes. Add garlic; sauté 1 minute. Stir in tomatoes and next 4 ingredients. Reduce heat to medium-low; cover and cook, stirring occasionally, 15 minutes or until vegetables are tender. Stir in basil, and serve immediately.

⤳ MARKET TIP ⤲

Farmstand fresh vegetables really shine in this
dish if you can get them. If not, frozen corn and limas
will work in a pinch.

Yellow Squash & Zucchini
GRATIN

This dish may sound fancy, but don't worry—a gratin is just a charming name for a vegetable casserole. Layered with slices of garden-ripe squash and zucchini and topped with Gruyère and breadcrumbs, this recipe will soon replace your go-to squash casserole dish.

serves: 4 ~ *hands-on:* 19 min. ~ *total:* 39 min.

Vegetable cooking spray

¼ cup butter, divided

2 medium zucchini, cut crosswise into ¼-inch-thick slices

2 medium yellow squash, cut crosswise into ¼-inch-thick slices

2 shallots, minced

2 garlic cloves, minced

½ tsp. kosher salt

½ tsp. freshly ground black pepper

¾ cup heavy cream

½ cup panko (Japanese breadcrumbs)

½ cup (2 oz.) freshly grated Parmesan cheese

1 oz. Gruyère cheese, shredded

1 tsp. chopped fresh thyme

1. Preheat oven to 450°. Lightly grease a 2-qt. baking dish with cooking spray. Melt 2 Tbsp. butter in a large skillet over medium heat; add zucchini and yellow squash. Cook, stirring occasionally, 7 minutes or until crisp-tender. Add shallots and garlic; sauté 1 minute. Stir in salt and pepper.

2. Spoon hot squash mixture into prepared baking dish. Pour cream over squash mixture.

3. Wipe skillet clean. Melt remaining 2 Tbsp. butter in skillet; add panko, cheeses, and thyme; toss to combine. Sprinkle breadcrumb mixture over squash mixture. Bake, uncovered, at 450° for 10 minutes or until top is golden. Let stand 10 minutes before serving.

MARKET TIP

Since this dish bakes for a short time (unlike a traditional squash casserole), the vegetables cook up fork-tender, not mushy or watery.

FRESH LIMA BEANS
with Sausage & Chili Flakes

We used to eat lima beans all the time growing up, but as I got older I found them tricky to find fresh. Now local farmers are bringing them to the markets, and they are easy to come by and so much better than their canned versions. Try them simply sautéed with sausage and a kick of spice.

serves: 4 ~ *hands-on:* 25 min. ~ *total:* 40 min.

1½ cups fresh baby lima beans

2 tsp. olive oil

½ medium onion, chopped

4 oz. ground pork sausage

1 garlic clove, minced

½ cup dry white wine

2 tsp. butter

½ tsp. kosher salt

¼ tsp. crushed red pepper flakes

¼ tsp. freshly ground black pepper

Garnish: fresh thyme leaves

1. Cook lima beans in a 3-qt. saucepan in boiling water to cover 15 minutes or until tender; drain.

2. Heat oil in a large skillet over medium heat. Add onion; cook, stirring occasionally, 5 minutes or until tender. Add sausage; cook, stirring to crumble, 4 minutes or until browned. Add garlic; cook, stirring constantly, 30 seconds. Add lima beans, wine, and next 4 ingredients; cook, stirring occasionally, 8 minutes or until liquid evaporates.

Peppered White Bean
MASH

This dish is an excellent side dish, but I also love serving it as an appetizer or snack to smear on some pita toasts or French bread with a drizzle of fruity olive oil.

serves: 4 ~ hands-on: 5 min. ~ total: 11 min.

2 Tbsp. olive oil, divided

2 garlic cloves, minced

1 Tbsp. chopped fresh thyme

1 Tbsp. fresh lemon juice (about 1 small lemon)

2 (19-oz.) cans cannellini beans, drained and rinsed

1 tsp. table salt

1 tsp. freshly ground black pepper

1. Heat 1 Tbsp. oil in a large skillet over medium heat. Add garlic, and sauté in hot oil 1 minute.

2. Add thyme, lemon juice, beans, and 1 cup water. Cook, stirring often, over medium heat 4 minutes or until thickened. Stir in salt and pepper, and place bean mixture into a large bowl. Mash with a potato masher, leaving some beans whole. Drizzle mash with remaining 1 Tbsp. oil.

Savory Twice-Baked
SWEET POTATOES

If you've only had sweet potatoes stuffed with brown sugar and marshmallows, you are in for a whole new experience. Crispy bacon, fresh chives, and a double dose of cheese turn these into the perfect savory accompaniment to a steak or even roasted turkey.

serves: 8 ~ *hands-on:* 13 min. ~ *total:* 1 hr., 33 min.

4 (¾- to 1-lb.) sweet potatoes

1 Tbsp. olive oil

½ cup (2 oz.) shredded Parmesan cheese

2 Tbsp. butter

2 Tbsp. chopped fresh chives

1 Tbsp. whipping cream

½ tsp. table salt

½ tsp. freshly ground black pepper

1 (3-oz.) goat cheese log, softened

4 hickory-smoked bacon slices, cooked and crumbled

Garnishes: crumbled goat cheese, chopped fresh chives

1. Preheat oven to 400°. Pierce potatoes all over with a fork. Rub potatoes with oil, and place on an aluminum foil–lined baking sheet; bake at 400° for 1 hour or until tender. Remove potatoes from oven, and reduce oven temperature to 350°.

2. Let potatoes stand until cool enough to handle. Cut potatoes in half lengthwise; scoop out pulp, leaving ¼-inch shells intact. Place pulp in a bowl; mash with a potato masher. Add Parmesan cheese and next 6 ingredients, mashing until smooth. Spoon potato mixture into shells; place shells on a baking sheet. Bake at 350° for 20 minutes or until thoroughly heated. Sprinkle with bacon.

WILD RICE SALAD
with Cranberries & Toasted Pecans

This recipe is inspired by my days of working in a sweet little restaurant called The Market Place in Huntsville, Alabama. I made a wild rice salad throughout the entire fall season that was unbelievably popular. This is my version of it, made with a fresh orange juice dressing and studded with cranberries and pecans. Now I serve it at my Thanksgiving dinner.

serves: 8 ~ *hands-on:* 13 min. ~ *total:* 1 hr., 3 min.

1 (6-oz.) jar wild rice

¾ tsp. table salt, divided

¼ cup fresh orange juice (1 orange)

3 Tbsp. chopped shallots

3 Tbsp. red wine vinegar

2 Tbsp. extra virgin olive oil

2 tsp. Dijon mustard

1 tsp. minced garlic

¼ tsp. freshly ground black pepper

¾ cup sweetened dried cranberries

½ cup chopped pecans, toasted

2 Tbsp. chopped fresh flat-leaf parsley

1. Bring 3 cups water to a boil in a large saucepan. Stir in rice and ½ tsp. salt; reduce heat, cover, and simmer 50 minutes or until rice is tender. Drain; rinse under cold running water, and drain. Place rice in a large bowl.

2. Whisk together orange juice, next 6 ingredients, and remaining ¼ tsp. salt in a small bowl until blended.

3. Add cranberries, pecans, and parsley to rice. Drizzle orange juice mixture over rice mixture; toss to coat. Serve immediately, or cover and chill until ready to serve.

Summer Corn
RISOTTO

This dish is not only a perfect accompaniment to a main course of grilled or roasted meats, but it is also hearty enough to stand on its own as a vegetarian entrée. Be sure to use fresh corn here—it makes a huge difference.

serves: 4-6 ~ *hands-on:* 43 min. ~ *total:* 43 min.

1 Tbsp. olive oil

1 Tbsp. butter

⅓ cup chopped shallots

3 garlic cloves, minced

1 cup Arborio rice

1 tsp. fresh thyme leaves

½ cup dry white wine

3½ cups vegetable broth

1 cup (4 oz.) shredded Parmesan cheese

1 cup fresh corn kernels (2 ears)

½ tsp. freshly ground black pepper

Garnish: chopped fresh thyme

1. Heat oil and butter in a large saucepan over medium heat until butter melts. Add shallots and garlic; cook, stirring occasionally, 2 minutes or until beginning to brown.

2. Stir in rice and thyme; cook, stirring constantly, 2 minutes. Add wine, stirring to loosen browned bits from bottom of pan. Reduce heat to low; simmer, stirring often, 1 minute.

3. Add 1 cup broth, and cook, stirring constantly, until liquid is absorbed. Repeat procedure with remaining broth, 1 cup at a time, ending with ½ cup broth. (Total cooking time is about 30 minutes.) Remove from heat.

4. Stir in cheese, corn, and pepper. Serve immediately.

Fresh Herb & Gruyère
BREAD PUDDING

Bread pudding isn't just a dessert. Made with cheeses and herbs, it's an excellent side dish for supper. It's also a great way to use leftover bread.

serves: 6 ~ *hands-on:* 13 min. ~ *total:* 1 hr., 3 min.

Butter

1½ cups milk

1½ cups half-and-half

¼ cup chopped fresh chervil

2 Tbsp. chopped fresh chives

1 Tbsp. chopped fresh dill

¾ tsp. table salt

½ tsp. freshly ground black pepper

5 large eggs

2 cups (8 oz.) shredded Gruyère cheese, divided

1 (12-oz.) French bread loaf, cut into 1-inch cubes

2 Tbsp. cold butter, cut into pieces

Garnishes: chopped fresh chives, chopped fresh dill

1. Preheat oven to 350°. Butter 6 (4-inch) ramekins.

2. Whisk together milk and next 7 ingredients in a large bowl. Stir in 1 cup cheese. Add bread cubes, stirring to coat. Pour bread mixture into prepared ramekins. Let stand 15 minutes. Sprinkle with remaining cheese, and dot with cold butter pieces.

3. Bake at 350° for 35 to 40 minutes or until golden and a wooden pick inserted in center comes out clean. Serve warm.

KITCHEN TIP

This recipe is ideal for making ahead. Just assemble through step 2, cover, and refrigerate. Before baking, remove from refrigerator and bring to room temperature.

Cornbread & Oyster
DRESSING

Dressing recipes can be very personal. I like mine with a mix of cornbread and French bread, but I know some people even use biscuits. I'm partial to oyster dressing, but you can easily leave out the oysters or replace them with 1½ cups browned sausage.

serves: 10-12 ~ *hands-on:* 23 min. ~ *total:* 1 hr., 8 min.

Butter

1 cup butter

1 medium onion, chopped

3 celery ribs, chopped

4 tsp. chopped fresh sage

2 tsp. Cajun seasoning

1 tsp. table salt

½ tsp. freshly ground black pepper

6 cups crumbled cornbread

6 cups cubed French bread, toasted and crumbled

2-3 cups chicken stock

2 pt. fresh standard oysters, drained and coarsely chopped

1 large egg, beaten

1. Preheat oven to 350°. Butter a 13- x 9-inch baking dish.

2. Melt 1 cup butter in a large skillet over medium heat. Add onion and celery, and sauté 5-6 minutes or until tender. Stir in sage and next 3 ingredients; sauté 1 minute. Remove skillet from heat.

3. Toss together cornbread and toasted bread in a large bowl; add vegetable mixture and 2-3 cups chicken stock.

4. Add oysters and egg, stirring gently. Spoon dressing into prepared dish. Bake, uncovered, at 350° for 45 minutes or until top is golden and crisp.

⤞ KITCHEN TIP ⤝

Adding only 2 cups of stock will result in a crisper dressing, while using 3 cups will make for a more bread pudding-like consistency.

Buttermilk & Green Onion
CORNBREAD

This is my go-to cornbread recipe. If you don't have a cast-iron skillet, here's a reason to get one. Cook a little bacon in it first, and then make my cornbread. The sizzling bacon grease creates the crunchy edges of this perfectly baked favorite.

serves: 8 ~ hands-on: 3 min. ~ total: 23 min.

2 tsp. bacon drippings

1¾ cups stone-ground cornmeal

1 tsp. baking powder

1 tsp. baking soda

1 tsp. table salt

1¾ cups buttermilk

1 large egg

½ cup finely chopped green onions
   (about 6 green onions)

Butter

1. Preheat oven to 450°. Place bacon drippings in a 10-inch cast-iron skillet. Heat skillet in oven 5 minutes.

2. Meanwhile, whisk together cornmeal and next 3 ingredients in a medium bowl. Make a well in center of dry mixture. Whisk together buttermilk and egg in a separate bowl.

3. Add buttermilk mixture to dry mixture, stirring just until moistened. Stir in chopped green onions.

4. Remove skillet from oven. Quickly tilt hot skillet in all directions so that bacon drippings cover bottom of skillet with a thin film; immediately pour batter into skillet. Bake at 450° for 20 minutes or until golden brown and cornbread pulls away from sides of skillet.

5. Invert cornbread onto a serving plate. Serve hot with butter.

Goat Cheese & Parmesan MUFFINS

Muffins might seem like a breakfast food, but not here. Present them in a bowl or basket wrapped in a linen napkin, and serve with some goat cheese instead of butter.

makes: 1 dozen ~ *hands-on:* 8 min. ~ *total:* 31 min.

Vegetable cooking spray

1½ cups all-purpose flour

2 tsp. baking powder

1½ tsp. sugar

¼ tsp. table salt

½ cup chopped green onions (about 3 onions)

2 Tbsp. milk

4 oz. goat cheese, softened

½ cup (2 oz.) freshly grated Parmesan cheese, divided

1 large egg, beaten

¾ cup milk

6 Tbsp. olive oil

1. Preheat oven to 400°. Lightly grease a (12-cup) muffin pan with cooking spray. Combine flour and next 3 ingredients in a large bowl. Stir in green onions; make a well in center of mixture.

2. Stir together 2 Tbsp. milk, goat cheese, and ¼ cup Parmesan cheese until blended. Stir in egg, ¾ cup milk, and oil; add to dry mixture, stirring just until moistened. Spoon batter evenly into prepared pan. Sprinkle evenly with remaining ¼ cup Parmesan cheese.

3. Bake at 400° for 18-20 minutes or until golden brown. Cool in pans on wire racks 5 minutes; remove from pans to wire racks. Serve warm.

NOTE: We tested with Belle Chèvre goat cheese.

Grilled Peaches

Homemade MOON Pies

Chapter
-6-
SOMETHING
Sweet

I have a confession to make: I don't really have a sweet tooth. Maybe that's an odd way to introduce dessert recipes, but then again, maybe not. The thing is, I like the idea of dessert. I guess you could say I get a rush from the sugar rush that I give others! My favorite desserts are simple things that make a big impact. Back in 2011, when tornadoes destroyed so many Alabama communities, our neighborhood lost power for days. During the day, we visited with neighbors we rarely saw under ordinary circumstances. We were all cooking and sharing food before it could spoil, and my son thought it was the best time ever. He didn't see the devastation—he saw the community. I remember that I had some apples and peaches—and a gas stove, fortunately—and I made little hand pies and fried them . . . in butter (let's not dwell on that part). Kelly loved them, so now I make them for him all the time. During that week when we had no conveniences but felt a personal connection with our neighbors, he said to me, "I want to live like this all the time!" I think about that when I make dessert. I want to serve something that will make friends and family think, "I want to feel this way all the time!" There's something here to satisfy every sweet tooth—and to inspire those of us who live for the smiles we see when we serve a truly memorable dessert.

Grilled
PEACHES

When peaches are in season from June through September, I like to prepare them on the grill, especially if my main course is made on the grill. It's a quick and simple way to serve fresh peaches without too much effort at all. They make a delicious dessert or even a sweet side to grilled pork.

serves: 7 ~ *hands-on:* 14 min. ~ *total:* 14 min.

7 peaches (about 2 lb.), halved and pitted*

2 Tbsp. olive oil

2 Tbsp. honey

Crème fraîche

1 Tbsp. finely chopped fresh mint

1. Preheat grill to 350°–400° (medium-high) heat. Drizzle peaches with oil. Place peaches, cut sides down, on cooking grate of grill. Grill, covered with grill lid, 3 minutes or until peaches are juicy and beginning to char.

2. Drizzle cut sides of peach halves with honey. Place a dollop of crème fraîche in the cavity of each peach half, and sprinkle with mint. Serve immediately.

*Large plums or nectarines may be substituted.

MARKET TIP

Overripe peaches will fall apart, so choose those that are ripe but still firm. The heat of the grill will soften them up even more.

RHUBARB GALETTE
with Chèvre Cream

I don't think rhubarb gets enough attention. I just love it and consider it a gift from the garden. This simple recipe really lets rhubarb shine paired with a little whipped goat cheese topping.

serves: 6 ~ *hands-on:* 10 min. ~ *total:* 2 hr., 50 min.

CRUST

1¼ cups all-purpose flour

1 Tbsp. sugar

¼ tsp. table salt

7 Tbsp. cold unsalted butter, cut into
 ½-inch cubes

4-5 Tbsp. ice water

Parchment paper

FILLING

1 lb. trimmed rhubarb, cut into ½-inch
 pieces

½ cup sugar, divided

½ tsp. vanilla extract

2 Tbsp. unsalted butter, cut into ½-inch
 cubes

1 large egg yolk, lightly beaten

TOPPING

4 oz. goat cheese, softened

¼ cup whipping cream

1 Tbsp. sugar

1. Prepare Crust: Whisk together first 3 ingredients in a medium bowl. Cut 7 Tbsp. butter cubes into flour mixture with a pastry blender until crumbly. Add 4 Tbsp. ice water; stir until dough clumps together, adding more ice water by teaspoonfuls if dough is dry. Gather dough into a ball; flatten into a disk. Wrap in plastic wrap, and chill at least 1 hour. Let dough stand at room temperature 10 minutes.

2. Meanwhile, prepare Filling: Combine rhubarb, 6 Tbsp. sugar, and vanilla in medium bowl; let stand 1 hour.

3. Preheat oven to 350°. Roll dough into a 12-inch circle on a large piece of parchment paper; transfer parchment paper with dough to a large baking sheet. Mound rhubarb mixture in center of dough using a slotted spoon. Fold dough border up and over filling, pleating as you go, leaving an opening 5 inches wide in center. Dot rhubarb mixture with 2 Tbsp. butter. Brush edges of dough with beaten egg yolk. Sprinkle galette with remaining 2 Tbsp. sugar.

4. Bake at 350° for 1 hour or until rhubarb is tender and juice is bubbly. Cool at least 30 minutes before serving.

5. Prepare Topping: Stir together all ingredients in a small bowl. Cut galette into wedges. Serve with goat cheese topping.

Peach FRIED PIES

Peach pies remind me of Alabama summers with my grand-mother. These portable desserts are great for summer picnics.

serves: 20 ~ *hands-on:* 55 min. ~ *total:* 2 hr., 1 min.

2 recipes Basic Pie Crust

Parchment paper

4 fresh peaches (about 1½ lb.)

3 Tbsp. all-purpose flour

3 Tbsp. granulated sugar

Dash of kosher salt

1 Tbsp. bourbon

½ tsp. vanilla extract

Peanut oil

½ cup powdered sugar

1 tsp. bourbon

1. Divide Basic Pie Crust dough in half. Roll each half of dough to ⅛-inch thickness on a lightly floured surface. Cut each half of dough into 10 (4¼-inch) circles, rerolling as needed. Transfer circles to a parchment paper–lined baking sheet; chill.

2. Peel and finely chop peaches. Combine peaches, flour, and next 2 ingredients in a bowl. Stir in 1 Tbsp. bourbon and vanilla.

3. Working with 10 dough circles, spoon 1 Tbsp. filling on half of each dough circle. Brush edges of circles with water. Fold dough over filling; gently press edges with a fork to seal. Return filled pies to baking sheet, and chill until ready to fry. Repeat procedure with remaining 10 dough circles and remaining peach filling.

4. Preheat oven to 200°. Pour oil to depth of 2 inches in a Dutch oven; heat to 350°. Fry pies, 5 at a time, 2½ minutes on each side or until golden. (Keep remaining pies in refrigerator until needed.) Drain on paper towels. Keep warm in oven.

5. Whisk together powdered sugar, 1 tsp. bourbon, and 1½ tsp. water in a small bowl until smooth. Drizzle glaze over pies.

Basic Pie Crust

makes: 2 (9-inch) or 8 (5-inch) mini pie crusts
hands-on: 6 min. ~ *total:* 1 hr., 6 min.

3¼ cups all-purpose flour

½ tsp. table salt

1½ cups cold unsalted butter, cut into small pieces

5-7 Tbsp. ice water

1. Pulse flour and salt in a food processor 3-4 times or until combined. Add butter, and pulse 5-6 times or until crumbly.

2. With processor running, add ice water, 1 Tbsp. at a time, just until dough forms a ball and pulls away from sides of bowl.

3. Shape dough into a ball. Wrap in plastic wrap, and chill 1 hour or until ready to use.

4. Roll to ⅛-inch thickness on a lightly floured surface according to recipe.

Phyllo Apple
HAND PIES

As much as I love a good fried pie, sometimes I'm not up for all the effort that goes into frying. That's when this recipe is the perfect go-to. Although these are baked, the phyllo dough makes them superbly flaky, and you can always find apples year-round. Serve with a scoop of ice cream on the side to make them even more indulgent.

serves: 12 ~ *hands-on:* 29 min. ~ *total:* 1 hr., 4 min.

2 tsp. butter

⅓ cup fine, dry breadcrumbs

3 Granny Smith apples (about 1½ lb.), peeled and cut into ½-inch cubes

1 Tbsp. fresh lemon juice (about 1 lemon)

6 Tbsp. sugar, divided

¾ tsp. ground cinnamon, divided

¼ tsp. ground ginger

⅛ tsp. ground cloves

20 frozen phyllo sheets, thawed, from 1 (16-oz.) package

½ cup melted butter

Parchment paper

Vanilla ice cream (optional)

1. Preheat oven to 350°. Melt 2 tsp. butter in a medium skillet over medium-high heat. Add breadcrumbs, and cook, stirring often, 2 minutes or until lightly browned. Remove from heat; cool 10 minutes.

2. Combine apple and lemon juice in a medium bowl. Stir together ¼ cup sugar, ½ tsp. cinnamon, ginger, and cloves in a small bowl. Add to apple mixture, and toss to coat.

3. Place 1 phyllo sheet on a flat work surface. (Keep remaining phyllo covered with a damp towel to prevent it from drying out.) Lightly brush sheet with melted butter. Top with another phyllo sheet, and lightly brush with melted butter. Repeat layering with 3 more phyllo sheets, brushing each sheet with melted butter. Cut phyllo stack in half lengthwise; cut crosswise into thirds, creating 6 (4½- x 4¼-inch) rectangles.

4. Spoon about 1 tsp. browned breadcrumbs into center of each rectangle; top with about 2 Tbsp. apple mixture. Fold 1 corner over filling to opposite corner of each rectangle, pressing edges to seal. Place on a baking sheet lined with parchment paper; cover with a damp towel. Repeat procedure with remaining phyllo sheets, melted butter, remaining browned breadcrumbs, and remaining apple mixture.

5. Stir together remaining 2 Tbsp. sugar and remaining ¼ tsp. cinnamon. Brush pies with remaining melted butter, and sprinkle with sugar-cinnamon mixture.

6. Bake at 350° for 20 minutes or until crust is golden brown and apples are tender. Cool on pan 5 minutes. Serve warm.

Pecan-Applesauce
COFFEE CAKE

When the family's in town, a comforting coffee cake always comes to the rescue for me. It's a sure crowd-pleaser—not surprisingly, because it's the best excuse to have dessert for breakfast!

serves: 16 ~ *hands-on:* 10 min. ~ *total:* 2 hr., 35 min.

CRUMB TOPPING

1 cup firmly packed light brown sugar

1 cup pecan halves, toasted and chopped

½ cup uncooked regular oats

½ cup cold unsalted butter, cut into pieces

1 tsp. ground cinnamon

½ tsp. table salt

CAKE

1 cup granulated sugar

½ cup firmly packed light brown sugar

½ cup unsalted butter, softened

3 large eggs

1½ cups unsweetened applesauce

1 cup sour cream

3 cups all-purpose flour

1 tsp. baking soda

½ tsp. table salt

1½ tsp. ground cinnamon

1 cup pecan halves, toasted and chopped

Unsalted butter

GLAZE

1½ cups powdered sugar

2½ Tbsp. buttermilk

½ tsp. vanilla extract

1. Prepare Crumb Topping: Using your hands, combine all ingredients in a medium bowl until mixture resembles small peas and is crumbly. Cover and chill until ready to use.

2. Prepare Cake: Preheat oven to 350°. In a large bowl, beat first 3 ingredients at medium speed with an electric mixer about 4 minutes or until fluffy. Add eggs, 1 at a time, beating just until blended after each addition. In a small bowl, combine applesauce and sour cream. In a medium bowl, combine flour and next 3 ingredients; add to butter mixture alternately with applesauce mixture, beginning and ending with flour mixture. Beat at low speed just until blended after each addition. Fold in 1 cup pecans.

3. Spoon half of batter into a buttered and floured 14-cup Bundt pan. Sprinkle with topping. Gently spread remaining half of batter over topping.

4. Bake at 350° for 1 hour and 10 minutes or until a long wooden pick inserted in center comes out clean, shielding with aluminum foil during last 10 minutes to prevent excessive browning. Cool in pan on a wire rack 15 minutes; remove from pan to wire rack, and cool completely (about 1 hour).

5. Prepare Glaze: Whisk together all ingredients in a medium bowl. Drizzle over cake.

MOON PIES

serves: 14 ~ *hands-on:* 23 min. ~ *total:* 3 hr., 55 min.

COOKIES

2 cups all-purpose flour

½ cup unsweetened cocoa

¼ cup cornstarch

1½ cups butter, softened

1½ cups powdered sugar

4 tsp. vanilla extract

MARSHMALLOW FILLING

1 envelope unflavored gelatin

2 Tbsp. cold water

2 large egg whites

¾ cup granulated sugar

¼ cup light corn syrup

¼ tsp. vanilla extract

CHOCOLATE COATING

24 oz. semisweet chocolate, chopped

½ cup vegetable oil

Parchment paper

1. Prepare Cookies: Stir together first 3 ingredients. Beat butter, powdered sugar, and 4 tsp. vanilla at medium speed with an electric mixer 2-3 minutes or until fluffy. Gradually add flour mixture, beating at low speed just until blended. Divide dough in half. Flatten each half into a ½-inch-thick disk. Wrap disks in plastic wrap; chill 1 hour.

2. Preheat oven to 375°. Unwrap 1 disk, and place on a lightly floured surface; roll to ⅛-inch thickness. Cut into 14 circles with a 3-inch round cutter dipped in flour; place 1 inch apart on a large ungreased baking sheet. Repeat procedure with remaining disk. Bake for 10 minutes or until crisp; cool 2 minutes on pans. Transfer to a wire rack, and cool completely.

3. Prepare Marshmallow Filling: Sprinkle gelatin over 2 Tbsp. cold water in a small bowl. Place egg whites in bowl of a heavy-duty electric stand mixer fitted with a whisk attachment.

4. Stir together granulated sugar, corn syrup, and ¼ cup water in a medium saucepan. Bring to a boil; wash down crystals from sides of pan with a small brush dipped in water. Cook, without stirring, until a candy thermometer registers 235° (about 5 minutes; lower heat as necessary to prevent mixture from boiling over).

5. Meanwhile, beat egg whites until soft peaks form. Remove sugar mixture from heat; add gelatin mixture, stirring until dissolved. Gradually add hot sugar mixture to egg whites, beating mixture at low speed, 30 seconds or until blended. Add ¼ tsp. vanilla. Increase speed to high, and beat 5-6 minutes or until mixture cools to room temperature and is thick but spreadable. Working quickly, spread filling on bottoms of 14 cookies. Top with remaining 14 cookies, bottom sides down. Place on a wire rack, and let stand 1 hour.

6. Prepare Chocolate Coating: In a medium glass bowl, microwave chocolate and oil at 30-second intervals, stirring often, until melted and smooth. Dip cookie sandwiches into hot chocolate. Place on a parchment-lined baking sheet. Chill until coating is firm.

Belle Chèvre Raspberry
TIRAMISÙ

Although tiramisù is traditionally made with mascarpone cheese, I prefer to use a honey-flavored goat cheese for the lightness and bright flavor it imparts. If you can't find it nearby, don't let that stop you from making this recipe—just stir a little honey into some fresh goat cheese.

serves: 5 ~ *hands-on:* 15 min. ~ *total:* 4 hr., 15 min.

1 cup hot espresso or hot strong brewed coffee

2 Tbsp. sugar

1 (6-oz.) container honey-flavored goat cheese

1 Tbsp. honey

¼ tsp. vanilla extract

1 cup heavy cream

1 (3.5-oz.) package crisp ladyfingers, broken in half crosswise

2 oz. semisweet chocolate, finely chopped

1½ cups fresh raspberries

Unsweetened cocoa

Garnish: fresh raspberries

1. Combine coffee and sugar in a 1-cup glass measuring cup, stirring until sugar dissolves.

2. Stir together cheese, honey, and vanilla in a small bowl until blended. Beat heavy cream until soft peaks form; gently fold in cheese mixture.

3. Dip half of ladyfinger halves in espresso mixture; place 4 ladyfinger halves in bottoms of 5 (10-oz.) ramekins. Sprinkle evenly with half of chocolate; top with half of raspberries. Spoon half of cheese mixture over raspberries, spreading evenly.

4. Dip remaining half of ladyfinger halves in espresso mixture; repeat layers, beginning with dipped ladyfinger halves and ending with cream mixture. Cover each ramekin with plastic wrap, and chill for at least 4 hours.

5. Unwrap ramekins; dust desserts lightly with cocoa. Serve cold.

NOTE: We tested with Belle Chèvre's Belle and The Bees Breakfast Cheese.

Banana Pudding
TRIFLE

As much as I like to put my own spin on most recipes, I believe that bananas shouldn't be messed around with too much. This recipe is simple and straightforward, but serving it up in a large glass trifle dish shows off all its glorious layers.

serves: 20 ~ *hands-on:* 23 min. ~ *total:* 3 hr., 23 min.

2½ cups sugar

6 Tbsp. all-purpose flour

Pinch of table salt

2 (12-oz.) cans evaporated milk

4 large egg yolks

¼ cup butter, cut into pieces

1 tsp. vanilla extract

1 (11-oz.) package vanilla wafers

5 bananas, sliced

Whipped Cream

Garnish: toasted coconut flakes

1. Whisk together first 3 ingredients in a medium saucepan. Gradually whisk in milk, and place over medium heat. Cook, whisking constantly, 7 minutes or until mixture comes to a boil; boil 1 minute or until thickened.

2. Whisk egg yolks until thick and pale. Gradually whisk about one-fourth of hot milk mixture into yolks; add yolk mixture to remaining hot milk mixture, whisking constantly. Place pan over medium-low heat, and cook, whisking constantly, 1 minute. Remove from heat, and add butter and vanilla, whisking until butter melts. Place heavy-duty plastic wrap directly on warm pudding (to prevent a film from forming); chill 3 hours. (Pudding will thicken as it cools.)

3. Layer one-fourth of vanilla wafers, banana slices, pudding, and Whipped Cream in a 4-qt. trifle dish. Repeat layers 3 times.

Whipped Cream

makes: 4 cups ~ *hands-on:* 3 min.
total: 3 min.

2 cups heavy cream

¼ cup powdered sugar

1 tsp. vanilla extract

1. Beat cream until foamy in a well-chilled bowl; gradually add powdered sugar and vanilla, beating until soft peaks form.

CHOCOLATE SHAKE
with Marshmallow Brûlée

Chocolate milkshakes bring the kid out in everyone. But this isn't just your average shake—this one is super special, topped with a handful of toasty, gooey marshmallows.

serves: 2 ~ *hands-on:* 5 min. ~ *total:* 5 min.

1 cup milk

2 Tbsp. chocolate syrup

2 cups chocolate ice cream

½ tsp. vanilla extract

¼ cup miniature marshmallows

1. Process all ingredients, except marshmallows, in a blender 30-60 seconds or until smooth. Pour into 2 tall dessert glasses.

2. Top each shake with 2 Tbsp. marshmallows. Toast marshmallows until tops are browned using a kitchen torch, holding torch 1-2 inches from marshmallows, and moving torch back and forth. Serve immediately.

KITCHEN TIP

Enjoy this frosty take on classic s'mores and serve with graham crackers for dipping.

Butter Pecan & Beer
FLOATS

With all the craft beers available today in almost any flavor you can imagine, I love pairing them with ice cream for my take on a float. Fruity beers go well with berry ice creams, while a chocolate stout balances nicely with a scoop of chocolate ice cream. This combination with pecan beer is one of my favorites.

serves: 4 ~ *hands-on:* 5 min. ~ *total:* 5 min.

1 pt. butter pecan ice cream

2 (12-oz.) bottles Southern pecan beer

1 Tbsp. finely chopped toasted pecans

1. Scoop ½ cup ice cream into each of 4 tall glasses; divide beer evenly among glasses. Sprinkle with pecans, and serve immediately.

NOTE: *We tested with Lazy Magnolia Southern Pecan Beer.*

Watermelon
GRANITA

Granita is just an Italian word for slushie or an icy dessert that couldn't be easier to make. You simply start with fresh watermelon juice that's sweetened, and then freeze it into fruity crystals of goodness.

serves: 6-8 ~ *hands-on:* 15 min. ~ *total:* 4 hr., 25 min.

4 cups cubed seedless watermelon

⅓ cup sugar

¼ cup loosely packed fresh mint leaves

2 Tbsp. fresh lime juice (about 1 lime)

½ tsp. lime zest

1. Process all ingredients in a blender until smooth; pour into a 9-inch square baking dish. Freeze mixture 1 hour. Stir, mashing any frozen parts with the back of a fork. Cover and freeze 3 hours or until completely frozen.

2. Let granita stand at room temperature 10 minutes. Scrape entire mixture with a fork to make large flakes. Serve in dessert dishes.

KITCHEN TIP

Watermelon Granita can be made up to 3 days ahead.
Cover tightly with aluminum foil, and keep frozen. Give it another
quick scrape to fluff it just before serving.

INDEX

METRIC EQUIVALENTS

The recipes that appear in this cookbook use the standard U.S. method for measuring liquid and dry or solid ingredients (teaspoons, tablespoons, and cups). The information on this chart is provided to help cooks outside the United States successfully use these recipes. All equivalents are approximate.

Metric Equivalents for Different Types of Ingredients

A standard cup measure of a dry or solid ingredient will vary in weight depending on the type of ingredient. A standard cup of liquid is the same volume for any type of liquid. Use the following chart when converting standard cup measures to grams (weight) or milliliters (volume).

Standard Cup	Fine Powder (ex. flour)	Grain (ex. rice)	Granular (ex. sugar)	Liquid Solids (ex. butter)	Liquid (ex. milk)
1	140 g	150 g	190 g	200 g	240 ml
¾	105 g	113 g	143 g	150 g	180 ml
⅔	93 g	100 g	125 g	133 g	160 ml
½	70 g	75 g	95 g	100 g	120 ml
⅓	47 g	50 g	63 g	67 g	80 ml
¼	35 g	38 g	48 g	50 g	60 ml
⅛	18 g	19 g	24 g	25 g	30 ml

Useful Equivalents for Dry Ingredients by Weight

(To convert ounces to grams, multiply the number of ounces by 30.)

1 oz	=	¹⁄₁₆ lb	=	30 g
4 oz	=	¼ lb	=	120 g
8 oz	=	½ lb	=	240 g
12 oz	=	¾ lb	=	360 g
16 oz	=	1 lb	=	480 g

Useful Equivalents for Length

(To convert inches to centimeters, multiply the number of inches by 2.5.)

1 in				=	2.5 cm		
6 in	=	½ ft		=	15 cm		
12 in	=	1 ft		=	30 cm		
36 in	=	3 ft	=	1 yd	=	90 cm	
40 in				=	100 cm	=	1 m

Useful Equivalents for Liquid Ingredients by Volume

¼ tsp						=	1 ml	
½ tsp						=	2 ml	
1 tsp						=	5 ml	
3 tsp	=	1 Tbsp			=	½ fl oz	=	15 ml
		2 Tbsp	=	⅛ cup	=	1 fl oz	=	30 ml
		4 Tbsp	=	¼ cup	=	2 fl oz	=	60 ml
		5⅓ Tbsp	=	⅓ cup	=	3 fl oz	=	80 ml
		8 Tbsp	=	½ cup	=	4 fl oz	=	120 ml
		10⅔ Tbsp	=	⅔ cup	=	5 fl oz	=	160 ml
		12 Tbsp	=	¾ cup	=	6 fl oz	=	180 ml
		16 Tbsp	=	1 cup	=	8 fl oz	=	240 ml
		1 pt	=	2 cups	=	16 fl oz	=	480 ml
		1 qt	=	4 cups	=	32 fl oz	=	960 ml
						33 fl oz	=	1000 ml = 1 l

Useful Equivalents for Cooking/Oven Temperatures

	Fahrenheit	Celsius	Gas Mark
Freeze water	32° F	0° C	
Room temperature	68° F	20° C	
Boil water	212° F	100° C	
Bake	325° F	160° C	3
	350° F	180° C	4
	375° F	190° C	5
	400° F	200° C	6
	425° F	220° C	7
	450° F	230° C	8
Broil			Grill

ISBN-13: 978-0-8487-4294-2
ISBN-10: 0-8487-4294-X
Library of Congress Control Number: 2014951569
Printed in the United States of America
First Printing 2015

Oxmoor House
Editorial Director: *Leah McLaughlin*
Creative Director: *Felicity Keane*
Art Director: *Christopher Rhoads*
Executive Photo Director: *Iain Bagwell*
Executive Food Director: *Grace Parisi*
Managing Editor: *Elizabeth Tyler Austin*
Assistant Managing Editor: *Jeanne de Lathouder*

Southern Living *Southern Made Fresh*
Editor: *Allison Cox Vasquez*
Senior Designer: *Shay McNamee*
Editorial Assistant: *April Smitherman*
Assistant Test Kitchen Manager: *Alyson Moreland Haynes*
Recipe Developers and Testers: *Tamara Goldis, Stefanie Maloney, Callie Nash, Karen Rankin, Wendy Treadwell, Leah Van Deren*
Food Stylists: *Victoria E. Cox, Margaret Monroe Dickey, Catherine Crowell Steele*
Photography Director: *Jim Bathie*
Senior Photographer: *Hélène Dujardin*
Senior Photo Stylists: *Kay E. Clarke, Mindi Shapiro Levine*
Senior Production Managers: *Greg Amason, Sue Chodakiewicz*

Contributors
Author: *Tasia Malakasis*
Designer: *Teresa Cole*
Writer: *Valerie Fraser Luesse*
Assistant Project Editor: *Megan Thompson Brown*
Junior Designers: *Frances Higginbotham, AnnaMaria Jacob*
Copy Editors: *Jacqueline Giovanelli, Rebecca Henderson*
Indexer: *Mary Ann Laurens*
Photographer: *Becky Luigart-Stayner*
Photographer Assistant: *Daniel Agee*
Photo Stylists: *Mary Clayton Carl, Lydia DeGaris Pursell*
Food Stylists: *Emily Nabors Hall, Erica Hopper*
Hair and Makeup: *Mary Beth Wetzle*
Fellows: *Laura Arnold, Kylie Dazzo, Nicole Fisher, Loren Lorenzo, Anna Ramia, Caroline Smith, Amanda Widis*

Time Home Entertainment Inc.
Publisher: *Margot Schupf*
Vice President, Finance: *Vandana Patel*
Executive Director, Marketing Services: *Carol Pittard*
Publishing Director: *Megan Pearlman*
Assistant General Counsel: *Simone Procas*